Tragedy
in the
Third World
Country:
The songs of Pain

Tragedy in the Third World Country:
The songs of Pain

CE. DEY

Order this book online at www.trafford.com
or email orders@trafford.com

Most Trafford titles are also available at major online book retailers.

Printed in the United States of America.

ISBN: 978-1-4269-7042-9 (sc)
ISBN: 978-1-4269-7043-6 (hc)
ISBN: 978-1-4269-7044-3 (e)

Library of Congress Control Number: 2011908191

Trafford rev.10/05/2011

 www.trafford.com

North America & International
toll-free: 1 888 232 4444 (USA & Canada)
phone: 250 383 6864 ◆ fax: 812 355 4082

Table of Contents

Acknowledgements

To all my grands, my dearest daughter, my Son wife and daughter. Also my brother. May God bless them.

Introduction

Ce Dey is a child of Guyana in South America – or – as this country is now called a new name – "the Guyana Republic." Her ancestors came from the countries of –

1) the Congo – Hence some of the families shorter statures.
2) Liberia – the inhabitants are noted for the heights
3) Nigeria – that part that is now called the Cameroon – they are noted for their strength, brilliance, good scholar – ships' standared, kindness, and gentility.

They came as captured slaves from Africa, and were brought to the countries of British Guyana – called in those days, as a colony belonging to London decades ago, under Victoria reign – in that era. These captives were given or divided between the Caribbean Islands, the three countries of French Guyana Dutch Guyana, and British Guyana, with British Guyana being the only English speaking country.

Ce's ancestors took their English given name, making it the equivalent of "Ruler" that name is now legally in past and future generations.

These ancestors were taught by their masters to read and to write. One of these great men, now educated was given the name "Doctor" by his people as he was taught to dispense medication and see to his people. Today after studying for the required degree the name "Pharmacist" was given to whomever passed that test. It was his people who gave him the name "Doctor."

He had other functions and work to perform, as also did some of the other handpicked men of our ancestors. They were tall, stalwart, handsome, gifted with lovely "Brown skin," which to this day is full of concert by others.

Later, after the abolishment of slavery by the "Queen of England," our ancestors, those that choose to remain in South America and the West Indies continued to maintain all their tribal customs, but this time joined them all together making this a very large joining of families. It is to these various matriarchs, patriarchs, of decades ago that Ce Dey has written this book in memory of their past struggles, outcomes, combining with the new eras and lives of these modern times.

I would always pay tribute to our hero's and heroines' for making our eras strong, very educated, passing their positive genes to us, the next generation/

Tragedy in a third world country – the Songs of Pain.

Dictionary –

chile, Fada	child, Father
Funeral Queh Queh	Creole songs for the deceased
Burial ground	cemetery
Grave yard	cemetery
coffin	casket
morgue	mortuary
clothes bats	Bats for beating, dirty wet clothing to become clean
yo, ya	you, your
yo Pickneys	your children
Pickneys	short for pickernene
Pickerneme	child or children of color
au, de	oh, the
appen	happen
trench	pond with flowing moving water

grande	Sister of Hilda Porta-Cops
Dutch Guyana culture	Burial on the eight day
British Guyana culture	Burial over, before or on the ninth day. If this is a first time for a mother with other children, this mother would skip the actual funeral and go to the burial site on the nine day.
Brook lax chocolate	For bowel activation. Looks like real chocolate, and to some people tastes the same. It also has a bitter tinge taste.
ga	go
wah da deh	what is that
libing	living for married life
gal	girl
yea, ah ha	yes; oh yes
run com ga	run along

Chapter 1

Washing Saturdays

It was down by the sea side
Very early on a Saturday morn
The village women came
To do their Laundering.

Baskets on they heads,
Ribbed boards for scrubbing,
And bats for beating their clothings,
Along with cakes of hard washing soaps.

This was like a picnic morning,
With the whole village running amock
Splash, Splash, scrub, scrub, rub, rub;
And much, much more.

Gossips flowing around the groups
Music playing, food for everyone
This was a typical Saturday,
By the side of the sea on the beach.

Today was Friday, the famous "planning Friday" as it was known. This was a day of hustlings, preparations, bakings, packing the clothing everything that goes with busy Saturdays. Oh, how these children enjoyed and loved these never ending weekends.

One would think this time of the week was like tin-pan alley, as the little ones scampered, and played, making their own instruments and beating bands, playing their own "mas bands" and bouncing in time with its rhythms.

The famous Saturday had arrived. The areas country folk never liked missing this agenda. Everyone came out to play in whatever areas they were comfortable with.

This was the day for big "to-do's." Lovely calypso bands, tight jeans, very short skirts, babies with bonnets and sun dresses to match, frilly laced panties, lace socks and minute dress shoes.

This was the day for the best dressers, faint at hearts, young lovers and those of all ages.

Then comes the stir up of crowds, namely 1) the musical rhythms of the steel bands; the thought of this causes one to sway, dancing on one's toes or jumping as the music says, "with hands in the air."

Sometimes the rumbling, gyrating tunes which draws your strength, while large groups of people keep swaying from side to side, singing in togetheriness "Tan, Tan," "Tan Tan," you then know that was the lovely tunes and rhythmic music of the great Byron Lee and the dragonaires. Oh, the sweet, sweet pounding of such breath taking body jerkings, sensational swinging rhythm-mix of the pounding bongoes in time and tunes, got you so confused in enjoyment, you suddenly found yourself adding new words to the newest persons of the now famous "Tan Tan," along with that would follow "bom bom," "bom, bom," and now a new song with music is formed. Work was forgotten some responsibilities, and a new experience arrives, along with another long word "Relaxation" for all.

The washing crowds came in droves and rows. –
With buckets
Scrubbing brushes,
hard soaps
Scrubbing boards,
Salt,
Lime,
bleach for the white clothes;

To start the ball rolling. These were for the way side washing, where all the juicy gossips of who was with whom;
All the pregnancies were listed, also – whom was beaten, and what punishments others received.

By now everyone at the Porta-Cops house hold were in wonderment, confusion, apprehension, and sadness. Something was going to happen. Something that was going to drain all of our energy. No one knew in what form these feelings would take as per Ms. Hilda
1) Would we be left listless,
2) Weak
3) and Lethargic
4) OR – would half of our young lives be no more.
suggestions were made all around in the household. One stuck heavily into their minds. With one accord, everyone fell and kissed the ground saying in turn: -

"We know not the future or what it brings to us. We only know it was sadness with very grave grief. We were running here, running there, running everywhere wondering who was leaving, leaving us now: -

[The Porta-Cops had strong Dutch ancestories, customs, beliefs and insites with feelings of dreads, unhappiness, grief and even joy also happiness.]

Oh! the pains of grief, the poundings of fear,
The closed eyes of streaming tears,
The pouting lips trying to withhold tearful sounds,
At least, at least, please give us a sign.

We know there would be losses by premonition feelings.
Such strong feelings, such strong fears.
We all know this was a sign from above

Which could be either way – "Positive or Negative."

The turn out of something good from something positive,
- OR – the presence of the toller of death
The negativity of that part is the bell tolleth for thee
We now know someone is departing, going from us, to the other side

Bang, Bang, Bang. There was a loud knocking on the front door of the Porta-Cop's home. Footsteps stomping up and down the steps;

Neighbors crying out, shrieking screams at the foot of Ms. Hilda Porta – Cops steps, gathering in large numbers, crying loudly in union "Lawd bad," Hilda-a-a-a, Hilda-a-a-le, trouble meet yo yard." "Yo pickneys them in trouble another voice said, "Miss Ilda, Ms. Ilda, Mo Ilda, are something bad done appen." "Come see ya pickney come"

Ms. Hilda Porta-Cops came and saw her precious twin babies being pulled out of the trench, their bodies list less, eyes closed, no breathing noted. They were unresponsive. They must have fell into that open water hours before the other children came out to play. They were both below the surface of the vast water floating in limbo.

Their bodies were pulled out across a long pole which was very thick. It took about four men to support the pole bean while the Porta-Cops children were pulled out.

These children were very close together, so the searching and seeking was quick in nature. They were taken out separately with limbs swinging and listless, their bodies hanging half over, and unconscious. No sign of life was noted.

Tears streaming down her cheeks, her voice could make no sound dear Ms. Hilda fell on her knees and collapsed into a heap gasping, pounding, screaming until she could do that no more. Saying to herself, and no one in particular.

They are mine, all mine.
They are mine, mine, mine.
No more please, no more
Take me, oh please take me.
My babies you must protect.
Take me in order that they would live.

With that Ms. Hilda crawled on her knees, going towards the listless, lifeless bodies of her two babies. She continued in the same flat, wounded tones –

No never alone, Oh never alone,
You promised never to leave my side
Please let this be the last.
Don't take them away from me
It would be a selfish thing to do.
You promised you'll never take them from me,
You'll never leave me alone.

This dear Grand mother continued her sad discant with refrain?? asking for the strength to face the future without the console and love from her babies. Again she whimpered in her fragile state –

I am nothing except a stranger in this land
Where I have encountered and faced dangers
Sorrow and bitterness surrounds me each day,
So in order to protect and save my children,
You could take me away with you.

Oh! Mother Porta-Cops could not be consoled this was a deep cutting wound. The lost of her two last babies, this sudden separation from her twins.

Mother Porta-Cops sat on her buttocks and ripped her blouse in half, her grief so profound, words could never express her feelings and hurt. She became very distraught.

What wrong was committed. Who wanted to hurt her so deeply, they took away her last two babies. Who grew this kind of hatred, harbored it into their hearts, and spew angrily its contents unto her.

Being of Dutch ancestors, mother Porta-Cops nervous and different from this her new habitation. She went back where she usually go in times of severe stress, upset, hurt and severe need. These influences brought the past into full circle again. She sat on her stool, book and pen in hand, and suspiciously made a list of all those who wanted to hurt her. She came to the name of "Carrot Demsley." This woman was very superstitious; believed in the occult, claimed to have strange powers, and could make bad things happen to anyone, who had, or unconsciously caused hurt, damage, danger, severe pain, have murderous thoughts, caused injury to her, her loved ones, and possessions.

When enquiries were made, Mother Porta-Cops had brought a picture that had great meaning to Ms. Carrot Demsley. This picture fell off the wall of the Demsley's resident while the children were playing outside the house of Ms. Demsley. The glass picture became broken into many pieces. To us younger ones we would call that the breaking – " into smitherines." These cracks, like the picture looked very sinister. The female in the picture looked hostile, angry, upset and felt mean and evil. No one knew what all of this signified, they only knew great fear, whenever one looked at that picture.

One Saturday morning Ms. Carrot Demsley came to the Porta-Cops demanding the return of her said picture that was destroyed. She wanted it to be well repaired, exactly as it was before, and ready to place into the special place on the wall.

Unknown to everyone Glen and Mark Porta-Cops saw the picture – its broken chipped glasses and faded picture, decided to dispose of everything. Without asking permission, the young male children threw the picture away into the dumpster. No one never knew, only an older cousin who was wiping the stairs, while the twins were going to the dumpster. When Ms. Carrot

Demsley arrived the grown ups looked for her picture which could not be found. The elder cousin acknowledged that said picture was thrown away.

At the children's death by accident – at the site Ms. Hilda collapsed singing while holding both children's head on either side of her lap as she rocked them with her chanting song –
Don't ever leave me
Don't ever say goodbye
I know that from the start
That we would love and never, never part

Oh please don't leave me,
Oh please do stay with me
You know I should be the one, to love
And leave you first.

So please remember
That I should be the one
To leave you first my dears
and prepare a place for you

Yes, you; y es you, ye – es you

Chapter 2

Mr. Carrot Demsley became so incensed after hearing this tale cried out into the air.

This is not happening to me,
This really is not happening,
These children are spoilt,
Having their own ways without redirections
Interfering with others' belongings
And not being taught to value others' properties.

Climbing down the stairs preparing to depart Ms. Carrot Demsley jumped around and said –

Some one has to pay.
Someone has to accept responsibility.
Something very personal to me was destroyed.
A possession that I have cherished.
Pain has to be felt with a deep hole into their hearts.
The cry of pain must be heard
Then and only then would my anger be subdued.

Nothing more was heard, seen, and known of or about Ms. Carrot Demsley. She had disappeared into thin air. Life went on as usual. Everyone was happy. The twins were behaving themselves.

Two months on a Saturday morning, while returning from the groceries, these children jumped out of the way of a car and into the deep trench for safety. This car never stopped but sped away leaving the dust to cover its tracks. These children completely forget they could not swim. They never came out alive.

Dear Ms. Hilda as she was sometimes called, continued in he collapsed state, whimpering and shaking her hands. This grievous shock causing her to be with pains all over her body said –

Oh! O-o-ooo-0000 the pain.
Who is this that did this deed
And took my kids from me.
This unplanned departure at this time
is sending a message to me.

Someone I may have hurt,
Who bears a vicious grudge,
have paid me back by taking my poots.
Oh death, Oh death, Oh death.
OH! ooo-ooo-000-oHo the pain of separation

Ms. Hilda was taken in a separate ambulance from the twins to the emergency room of the local hospital. The news spread everywhere, as the Porta-Cops were very important in the community. As the news spread everyone gathered and congregated. There were the aunts, uncles; First, Second, and third cousins, schoolmates, Godparents and other extended family members.

There were screams, faintings, pounding of the walls of the hospital, everyone very distraught. One elderly first cousin said–

"This sounds like Rachael weeping for her kids because they were no more." Aunt Margaret the children's older and most senior relative said –

"We must all cry with faith, and grieve with gratitude for the time these babies had lived here on earth. Never ask the question why; just say his will was carried out and they are safe. They were well appreciated and a joy to all. They did not suffer, but went instantly.

Dear old grande, the children's grand-aunt, and their grand-mother's sister cried saying –

"The lost of my grands has turned me into an aged person. Please let me see them just one more time, to be sure they are now no more.

With tears flowing down her cheeks, Dear Grande said –
My babies have left mehurriedly, without –
   a) a kiss,
   b) hug
   c) and a wave of good-bye
She then continued –

Why the hurry, dear children of mine.
Why the haste to go away.
Twelve years you spent with us down here,
and now you are no more.
Twelve years of hugs and squeezes,
Now they are no more.
Such a short time we spent together,
Now you have gone without a word,
And now it is good-bye my dears, good-bye,
Good-bye, good-bye, good-bye.

Every one went away slowly, the others then decided to pay a visit to Hilda Porta-Cops, as she was admitted to the hospital.

Am I dreaming she said. Did I hear them just right. Have my babies departed. Were they not saved. I can hear them calling me, and yet they are no more.

They are scared, frightened, and have no one with them.

They need their mother, a hug, and support,
My babies are calling me over to them.

Families came from all over the country and the globe.
There were those from some of the continents.
This was a very large family.

They were close, supportive towards each other and very generous.

Ms. Hilda Porta-Cops was sent home the next day. Relatives brought –
   1) large bags of food.
   2) two cows were killed for this sad preparation.
   3) a pig – one very large
   4) goat – two
   5) sheep – one
These were for the preparations of –
   1) Seven days of mourning on the Dutch side of the family.
   2) Nine days total being – nine days in all to mourn, until the ninth night.
All the local families' homes were filled to capacity with relatives and friends from afar.

On the first night Cousin Cleo – a second cousin became upset and exclaimed – "This food is taking forever. I am starving. This protest continued until her four young children and herself were served. She made them ate their full cousin Cleo later showed her anger saying – this sliced meat was not enough to feed an army. She then accepted a larger second helping with one very larger steak at the side of her plate. For the balance of that first night cousin Cleo was quiet and contented.

Chapter 3

Along came great Aunt Vetty. At eighty-seven years younger, she still had a strong voice, sang alto in church. Hates it when the young family members departs, or – as per her are called away. She was called by all "Dearest Aunt V." As she approached the steps one can hear her chanting in her discant alto voice.

"Yes! He's called the dear children.
Suffer them not, Let them go in peace.
Today this family suffered a terrible tragedy.
Now we must cry, cry and cry again.
For our children of twelve years old,
Were taken away because they were needed.
So go dear babies, we really did love you,
But you were loved best, so you must go."

Dearest Aunt V cried to break her heart. She was settled, made comfortable, and of course fussed over. This senior matriarch took her pen and note book to begin her assignment duties of all family members. The point was each family knew their jobs long before such occasions arose.
This list began with –
  1) Flowers – the Family's name who was in charge of this.
  2) Program for burial
  3) Looking after quarter of the guest x four houses
  4) Cookers x 4 houses
  5) Feeders x 4 houses
  6) House cleaners x 4 houses
  7) Clothes shopping – four family members for the other
  8) Dressing the deceased times two
  9) Clothing for the deceased x 2
  10) Looking after the children x four houses

11) Looking after the senior members of the family x four houses

12) Family nurses x 4 houses

Dearest Aunt V then promised to give briefings to everyone. She was the family's spokesperson.

Ms. Hilda, the children's mother continued to be heavily sedated. She was not doing well at all.

The villagers stopped all their activities for that5 day and went on with their grievings. Everything went haywire. From always being a big day in the country the famous "Washing Saturdays" along with different area parties, music and happiness were postponed gone for the time being were the

1) Gathering and separating of clothes, example.
   a) White separates
   b) Colors separates
   c) Very dark colors separates
2) Clothes bats for beating the dirt out of the clothing
3) Hand brushes to use both hard soaps on the clothings
4) Scrubbing boards for scrubbing the clothes
5) Hard soaps – these are special soaps. These are good for cloth washings. They do not form suds. They are good for any types of water. Tide box soaps were also used.
6) Plastic aprons to protect the clothing they were wearing.
7) Baskets with clothes to wash
8) Music boxes and heads of tapes marked with its owner's names
9) Picnic foods, plates, cutlery, glasses and sodas. This was a special time for children. A kind of bonding for working families, also anyone with and without children. As everything in the country, this really was a multi colored affair. That day was spoilt by this tragic event.

The children had lost both parents years ago after an outbreak of Typhoid fever at another village. Hilda Porta-Cops took over their grooming education, and everything. She became the sole provider for the twins.

Ms. Hilda always had children staying with her at some time or another. She → Ms. Hilda gave birth to three children who all went over, before her, the last one to leave was the twins mother. She even changed her grands surnames to hers by law. She had left the children's surname → Simpson, and were then called – Simpson-Porta-Cops, thus having both parents surnames.

Ms. Hilda was a single parent, having lost her husband during World War. She was a very strong lady, with good convictions, religious background, educated and extremely kind. She was known for having the neighborhood children in her home, feeling and caring for them. Her home was always full of lively children playing merrily, happily and joyfully. Now losing her last two babies was like also losing her daughter "Pat" all over again. The children were about two years when their parents had departed. Now ten years later her daughter and husband have returned for their children. They had loaned them for a little while, so they could be appreciated and loved by all. Now as per Ms. Hilda she said –

Dearest lovely Pat; my gracious daughter, you loaned them to me for such a short time, twelve years is still too short for me. I realized eventually you would collect them. Now my children rest in peace.

Place your heads on your mother's breast.
Always remember the love you were taught,
Also the love you shared with each other.
So good-bye my dear babies,
Goodbye my loving children.
Just hold each other's hands
and gently fade away.

Dear Hilda spent the third day crying, while making things ready for her babies departure. She was a great seamstress. Each stitch she said was carried out with love, love from a mother to her departing babies.

Hilda had decided to have an early night as the next day was a busy day, as only the Dutch would understand. Ms. Hilda was really a stickler for protocol and principles. Her country's customs were foremost always in her mind, and would do everything to maintain her countries customs.

On the fourth day Ms. Hilda decided on two things –
1) The post mortem of her two children
2) The ruling from the courts

The courts claimed her babies were killed by person or persons unknown. The case was left open for quite a while. The investigation had continued without success.

Chapter 4

The gatherings continued. On the fifth night, some family members decided to sing some hymns with the piano.

1) Some were crying, while others were –
2) praying
3) eating
4) cooking

The children were asking questions, but were not receiving any answers to please them.

While singing a new hymn –

"Let the stranger in," the police were knocking at the door. After inquiring what was the reason for the noise, the head of the household were advised to lower the noise and singing. They were very sympathetic towards Ms. Hilda.

Our own cousin Cleo was still on the warpath for food and other comforts. You heard things like – "snapping her tongues loudly she would burst out at intervals, to no one in particular." Very little meat and very little food." she then continued loudly. "Can I have more peas and rice, with a large amount of meat." To themselves the younger family members said – "Oh dear, what a way Cousin Cleo is greedy." After snapping her tongue saying the food was delicious, she now criticizes the amount of everything she had received.

The house was packed with late arrivals, coming with

1) greetings
2) gifts of food
3) cash money
4) drinks, sodas, and alcohol
5) games
6) sympathy cards

7) helpers

The children were in another family house playing

1) music
2) hip hop
3) dancing
4) reading
5) and singing

Everyone was grieving in their own way –

1) there were the large eaters
2) singers
3) dancers
4) criers
5) story tellers about long ago and far away. The passing
6) prayers

Everyone was occupied.

One of the younger aunts "Aunt Winnie Goodyear" known to the children and the younger generation as "Aunt Winnie" said; "one thing about deaths, you see every side of everyone." You get –

1) Lots to eat
2) Plenty of single men. Most need comforting. As Aunt Winnie would say – "You could feel the need and with a smirk on her lips, she would continue. I am here to help them all with their grieving. I could see the need during their sad periods of mourning.

Mother Earls and her two daughters – "Onie and Tonie" supervised the cleaning of the houses and everyone's needs.

Sister Ray – did the cooking along with the Hottrots family, their names were – Jean, Pan Co. and Ponk.

There were always lots to eat. Hot fresh foods, and dishes that the travelers might never have heard of.

The young Ms. Hope was master of all trades. She became everyone's helper, advisor, and problem solver.

With all the confusion that was going on no one thought about protecting the valuables of the homes.

The families were well off, and had a lot of treasures. Very expensive, delicate to the touch, fragile and lots of antiques.

Days six and seven were like ocean waves. Mood swings affected everyone.

Breakfast was early. Jobs were waiting for everyone. Everything went great until the evening of the sixth night. Machines were busy with sewing of clothings. Almost everyone had something to try on.

The nutritious foods with its enticing aroma, had everyone pacing, waiting for the mouth watering delicacies to arrive.

Suddenly the smell of this good cooking was wearing away, when Ms. Cleo inquired about the sharing of dinner.

Going into the kitchen everyone suddenly realized those extremely two large pots had disappeared. The fires were still going.

Due to the largeness of the pots, the old coal burners were used outside the back of the yard by the steps of the back door. this had to be the job of more than one person. Ms. Daisy placed her head to inquire where the pots were. No one could answer. There was a big search for the pots. For example –

1) Under the cupboard
2) Behind the outside steps
3) At the back of the house where the kitchen was situated for this occasion

No one could understand where these two big pots of food consisting of –

a) One pot of cook-up rice including in the pot a cut up tripe.
b) Salted beef – the salt had to be boiled out
c) Salted pigtail – the salt had to be boiled out
d) Peas

e) Seasonings along with a large amount of married man pork – this is a special seasoning that gives the food as per grand – "a good kick"
f) Thick thyme seasonings
g) Shallots
h) Onions and garlic
i) Black eye peas – boiled and soft
j) Rice about eight pints of rice
k) Meat – or – cows meat – or beef – well seasoned about eight pounds
l) Milk from three grated coconuts

Everything was divided in half. These pots were big enough to feed two army of soldiers.

Neither the pots nor the food were ever found. Someone was going to have a big after party. Some of the drinks from the continent of Europe and America also disappeared. Oh! Dear Grand Nana who had kept quiet until now said –

"There are dishonest family and friends around us." Grand Nana looked around and then said – Be true to yourselves dear families, we are hurting enough these days. So please be kind and stop hurting each other. At least until the grieving moments cycle is finished.

Tomorrow we are placing our loved ones to rest. Let us spend this last day with them, in peace. Love, unity, and harmony as they will be no more. We have always loved them, even to the extremes of spoiling them a little.

So our caring children big and small, no more blame, let that rest, and spend the time with more love to give, kindness and charity. As it is at home our charities must begin.

Still in her mourning stance Mother Porta – Cops continued with her singing – Pleading with her children not to leave her. Crying out a mother's job is to prepare a place for them. How could they do that to her.
The calling –

Oh-o-o-o how could you e-e-ver leave my-y side.
Without a word or thought
Oh how could you do that
In such a hu-r-ry to depart.

An-n-n-nd the pain th-at this ha-as caused.
Is so un-bea-ra-ble.
This sud-den pain would ne-ver stop.
My loving lit-tle ones.

You should ne-ver rush o-oh no
You ne-ver should, oh you never should
Yes the ca-al-ling came ea-r-ly.
Its over now – yes – its o-ver now.

Chapter 5

Ms. Hilda kept to herself most of the next couple of days. She was very isolative. Everyone was becoming concerned. She was discharged home from the hospital on the very next day after the incident. Ms. Hilda suddenly jumped up from her bed early on the seventh day.

This day was special – it is the Post Mortem day, time being ten o'clock in the morning. Also the last day before the funeral on the eight day.

Oh! Oh!! Oh!!! Help! Help! Help, hellllp.
What is this I am hearing.
My children are gone, all two of them
OH! help me; Help me; Help me-e-e-e-e-e.
Now there is no money to bury the dead.
What a shame; What a shame, shame, shameee

Everyone entered into her room. She received comfort from everyone. Ms. Hilda was given hugs, cuddles, kisses along with many more tears from everyone.

Unknown to Ms. Hilda everything was settled by the families.

The funeral home due to the tragedy decided not to charge nor bill for the entire funeral. Everything was covered.

No one could subdue Ms. Hilda. Her private doctor came immediately and medicated her with an injection of valium five milligrams intramuscular to be repeated in four hours. Also to inform the doctor of her progress. If third dosage needed to call the doctor again.

There were nurses in the family, so one volunteered to administered the correct dosage. They were all licensed in the area of the incident.

On this seventh night, everyone had hoped for an early night.

Out of no-where came Ms. Shelia a cousin of long standing, who was accustomed of having her laxative, never mind where she goes. She would complain of the usual stomach ache. Looking for her chocolate of brooklax which became lost in the crowds of relatives and children.

This make believe packet of chocolate resembled a Cadbury's plain packet. Knowing that children were around everywhere in droves, some of the adults decided to confront the children. Ms. Shelia asked the first question. She began –

Oh children what have you done
You have taken something
That would never, ever become a child's treasure,
and classified as sweet things to eat.

Some has eaten something that looks like a cocoa slab.
This if eaten could harm and cause severe damage. The outcome of which could be very disastrous. Someone would be very ill before the night is over.

So please, please, dear babies of ours.
Admit to your wrong, and all would be well. Admit to your error and we would look after you. You are our babies, we want you saved.

The children as usual stood stoned face and wondered, wondered what they were all thinking and talking about. The color of this missing piece was described as looking like a chocolate, tastes like one, but it is medication. We would know who has taken this before the night is out. These brats all replied. "Are you sure Auntie," about everything, and the piece of broaklax chocolate." Out of the blue little precious Demsley ten years said, "Oh Auntie is greedy trying to take all that chocolate for herself. She is not sharing," greedy Auntie. Everyone was laughing. Little Demsley was always up to tricks, but as she denied vehemently taking the brooklax. All everyone could do at this time was to sit and wait it out. The adults decided to take turns throughout the night, waiting in case help was needed.

Around one o'clock in the morning, there was flushings and continuous flushings, also groans followed. This continued plus a groaning. "Everyone dashed to the bathrooms, there was our precious and a bigger cousin Queenie 14 years old. Little Demsley was sitting on the toilet.

1) Skin cold and clammy
2) Bedclothes soaking wet
3) In every pore there was perspiration dripping out of her body. Sheets and blankets were wrapped around this little pumpkin and taken to the hospital immediately.

Queen the second cousin we also covered in a sheet and blanket. They both went to the emergency room and admitted.

They were both on the pediatric unit of the hospital. Intravenous fluids were ordered for them, to run every eight hours into their veins so that these children could regain their lost body fluids. Also medication to stop the liquid diarrhea they were having. This diarrhea was typical to ordinary stool, and was watery due to laxative ingestion.

These babies did admit to taking half each of the laxative. They spent one week in the general hospital. The funeral was out for them. The nurses spoil them rotten. They were upset, not about the funeral, but for the exercises that the family children were taught to perform, as they were in the limelight. Their mother's also stayed with them on the day of the funeral.

Mother Earlyn Core and her two daughters Ann and Theresa offered to stay at the homes during the funeral on the eight day.

Whatever was performed for the first seven days was very hush, hush. No children were involved. Only four of the adults who were very faithful to their mother country "Dutch Guyana."

It was a known fact that things got stolen from homes, once the funeral dates, times and the empty homes were made known. All belongings appeared to be accounted for at this time. Everyone went to bid farewell. Some stayed, some started packing and preparing for departure. Those who were living near went to their homes.

This was the ninth day after death. This day after a light lunch, homeward bound was everyones plan.

Chapter 6

The Porta cops home was prepared for the arrival of the bodies of her children from the Mortuary.

Ms. Hilda besides owning a mansion also came from a very large prestigious, and well to do family background. They were also very educated.

Aunt V besides being the seamstress for the children, was also one of the elected dressers.

Having a strong creole background, half Dutch, and children of slaves, they all had a little of every departure songs for this situation.

The twins atire consisted of –
1) Blue navy suits
2) Light blue shirts
3) Ties to match their blue suits

Their lapel suit pockets had small light blue handkerchiefs each.

4) Their coffins – light in color was also lined with light blue to match their shirts
5) Their under clothings were all white with socks and blue male slippers to match their suits

These twelve year olds were going to be put away with class; the area for the coffins had blue carnations in various bunches, along with green leaves, the walls of that area was painted with a combination of white and blue mixed. The flooring was covered with navy blue linoleum. The place looked like a King's castle.

The horses were arriving with the twins. This was a very sad time for all. The families and children formed lines as they were taught. The boys and senior males on the left hand; the girls and senior females on the right hand. "Aunt V" and "Uncle Jobe" led the procession to greet the arrivals. Their strong alto, bass, high soprano voices could be heard with the ancestral passing song.

Grandma Porta Cops was placed to sit in an area around her coffins. Greeting the arrivals you hear Aunt V's strong alto –

Oh Sina dey
Rainey ah co co
Rainey ah co co, ah co, ah co
Rainey ah co co
Oh Sina dey
Rainey ah co co.

They never stopped chanting this slavery death Quek, Quek until everything was fixed and situated.

The horses arrived around three o'clock. The service commenced at four in the afternoon and ended at five-thirty o'clock in the same day, with their school friends marching towards the cemetery, so the boys could be laid to rest. The program was made by the familys' poet/song writer Aunt Kathie –
The PROGRAM –

Marching procession headed by Reverent Joyce Marone, M.D.

The Lord's Prayer	Sung by Aunt Katie
Jesus Loves the Little Children	Ten younger children – friends
Lead me Gentle Home	Ten little cousins
Jesu, Joy of Man's Desiring	Sr. male members of family
The 23rd Psalm – sung	Aunt V
Oh Lovely Peace	Sr. female members of family
Obituary	Aunt Kathie
The 25th Psalm reading	Congregation, Verse 7
Sermon and praise reading	Reverent Joyce Marone, M.D.
Speed Bonny Boat-departure	School children – 20
Closing prayer	Reverent Joyce Marone

The Front of the Program –
Farewell greetings to our babies
"A drawing of our babies"
Date-of-Birth- June 3rd, 1933
Then departure time, 7 pm   Date December 1st, 1945
Address for function to end

Their new residence – "Back dam Cemetery in 62 Courentine
Berbice.

At the back of the program – the last page –
Thanking everyone for their support.

At the end of the service, the school children were place in rows
of threes.
Marching to the final resting place; led by Auntie Kathie and the
school children and other friends and families.
Marching –
We are marching to Zion,
Beautiful, beautiful Zion
We're marching onward to Zion
The beautiful city of God.
This was sung continuously to their final resting place.
Seeing this large procession marching with this hymn brought
tears to one's eyes. Indeed they marched to Zion.
At the ground the whaling of the Creole families Quek, Quek for
all occasions – sung to welcome the coffins to their new resting
place.
At the ground "Aunt V" commenced her descant as the horses
stopped along with bongos, heavy base from the older men.
Oh Sina day
Rainey ah co co.
Rainey ah co co, ah co, ah co.
Rainey ah co co.
Oh Sina dey

Rainey oh co co.

The coffins were removed the mourning soulful tunes continued until they arrived in front of their final resting place. The entire area and everyone became very quiet.

Cards of appreciations to a long list of people and everyone who helped this family in their grief.

1) Special thank you were said to the villages for assisting Mother Porta-Cops in her raising of her mom-grande
2) Special thanks to the Police Chief and his staff.
3) The Doctors, nurses and other hospital staff.
4) The principal, teachers, and children of their school.
5) The church ministers, neighbors and every known and unknown persons.
6) The funeral home for all their support

A few words from Auntie Reeme –

You have left us without a sound.

Yet we knew it was not in anger.

We will always remember the happiness you did leave us with.

And also the bitter-sweet memories

that we have received.

You are now with your parents

So good-bye our sweet ones, good-bye.

This was mostly a children's affair. All the children took part. This was a singing family. The minister was also a family member. The twins great Aunt – her name was "the very reverent Joyce Marone.

The children marched to the burial ground behind the horses with Auntie Kathie singing with the children – We're marching to Zion.

The burial ground was not very far from the Port-Cops residence. This was a short walk. A block from the burial site, "Aunt V" came out of the family's mourning car and for the third time in three days 'Aunt V' raised in song in her famous alto/descant words from long ago, from her native country, this daughter from a slave, with her haunting eyes started with their song of yesteryear." Oh Sine dey, "It was as if the world was coming to a sad end. In one side you hear the men in base, females in soprano high voices and the children – this new growth of fresh voices that melted with the evening air pulled every feelings, strengths, melodious renditions out of everyone. It was so intense, even the men of the village had tears running down their cheeks. This intensity and heavy sadness never stopped until every thing was settled at the grave site. This warbling reminded one of the sad times during slavery, when singing appears to sooth the brows, and even the savage beast in some of our relatives. The moving, walking antics, the slavery actions as this loss was told in song and music was a site to behold 'Aunt V' our song bird out did herself this time; the "Oku" in her came out.

The twins were placed side by side and entombed. They were not allowed near their parents due to the infections their parents had passed away from, their parents side of the entombment would finally be joined with other family members, but no one would be placed on their parents that would also be an extension of their family plot. Ms. Porta-Cops on seeing her mom-grands entombed, stood up from her portable chair and belted out one of the saddest refrains that anyone has ever heard sang again "Oh lovely peace." This tored at one's soul. After managing to quiet her for a while, so she could be transported home, Ms. Hilda the grieving Mom-Grand started singing softly with tears pouring down her face and cheeks, eyes closed, head shaking tried paying a final homage to her precious babies, their favorite song – Speed Bonny boat like a bird on the wing.

With that Dear old Hilda collapsed on the ground among the grass and flowers in the graveyard area the males in her family rushed to her side. Muscular Ian picked her up and gently kept her in his arms, cuddling her like a baby, kissing her cheeks, and forehead, treating her as she did to him when he was hurting as a child.

An invitation of Love and Praise

Place – the Porta Cops Residence

Address -   62 Courentyne
                Berbice
                British Guyana
                South America

You are invited to our children's joyous and successful journey –
as they go to join there parents.

Date of departure started – June 3rd, 1944 –
Travels ended – 1945 – December 1st.
Time of arrival – 7 pm to join their family at home.

Go my beloved children Go,
For your Ma and Pa are awaiting
your arrivals.

Their invitation of burial.

The Lord's Prayer

Our Father who art in heaven
Hallowed be thy Name
Thy Kingdom come,
Thy will be done on earth as it is in Heaven.

Give us this day our daily bread
And forgive us our trespasses
As we forgive those who trespass against us.

And lead us not into temptation,
But deliver us from evil
For thine is the Kingdom and the Glory.
Forever. A-men.

Jesus loves the little children
Jesus loves the little children
Above the bright blue sky
A love that never faileth
A love that never die
No other man is like him
Or like him can compare
This one is always worthy
In his great name we praise.

This was a Sunday favorite of Ms. Hilda and her children. After church its talking time about their parents. That always ends with Jesus loves the little children.

Lead me gentle home
Lead me gentle home father
Lead me gentle home
There to last forever
From all earthly sins
Least I fall upon the wayside
Lead me gently, gently home.

Lead me gently
Home Father lest I roam
Upon the wayside
Lead me gently – gently home

Oh lead me gent-ly ho—me.

Bringing tears to everyone's eyes. These 10 little cousins, friends and God – brothers sang and brought the congregation to their feet.

Jesu, Joy of Man's Desiring

Jesu, joy of man's desiring
Holy wisdom love most bright.
Drawn by thee, our souls aspiring
Soar to uncreated light.
Word of God, our flesh that fashioned.
With the fire of life impassioned,
Striving still to truth unknown,
Soaring, dying round thy throne.

Through the way where hope is guiding,
Hark, what peaceful music rings,
Where the flock, in thee confiding,
Drink of joy from death less springs.
Theirs is beauty's fairest pleasure,
Theirs is wisdom's holiest treasure.
Thou dost ever lead thine own
In the love of joys unknown

Music by J. S. Bach

The senior male members of the family sang this moving rendition. The congregation was lifted.

The Lords my Shepherd – 23rd Psalm
The Lords my Shepherd
I'll not want, he makes me down to be.
In pastures green he leadth me
The quiet waters by.
In pastures green, he leadth me.
The quiet waters by.

Yea though I walk through
deaths dark vale
yet may I fear no ill
For thou art with me, and thy rod.
and staff me comfort still
For thou art with me, and thy rod,
And staff me comfort still.

Mother Porter Cops taught her children this hymn after their mother Pat and father passed away during a typhoid epidemic. They always felt very close to their natural parents with this.

by Aunt V

Oh Lovely Peace
Oh lovely peace with plenty calm
Oh Lovely, lovely peace.
Come Spread thy blessings
Thy blessings all around.

Oh Lovely peace
Oh lovely, lovely peace
Let fleece flocks the hills adore
And valleys smile with wavery corn.

Let fleece flocks the hills adore
And valleys smile with wavery corn
And valleys smile with wavery corn
And smile with wavery corn,
With wavery corn, with wavery corn, with wavery corn.

This touched the hearts of many. To sooth her babies Ms. Hilda always settled with this song. This was fitting for this occasion.

by Senior Family members

Obituary
Our blessed children Glen and Mark Simpson – Porta-Cops were given to our family from the Lord. Treasures that we all adored. They became mine as my children and also grand-children. Their parents left us when my darlings were two years old. These loving duo looked after and cared for their mom-grand and other senior family's.

Left to mourn – their mom-grand, Aunt V, Aunt Katie and a host of other grands great grands, cousins, multiple friends, loving teachers, and the village that took to raise our twins.

by Aunt Katie

Proverbs 25 – Verse 7
For it is better that he say to you, "Come up here: than that you should be put lower in the presence of the Prince, whom your eyes have seen.

The Congregation

Closing Prayer
Now lettest thy servants depart Oh Lord, according to thy will in peace.
Give their spirits peace Lord forever – A-men.

By Reverend Joyce Marone

Speed Bonny Boat
Speed Bonny Boat like a bird on the wing
Onwards the sailors cried
Carry the lad that's born to be King
Over the sea to skye.

Loud the winds howled
Loud the winds rolled
Thunder claps rend the air
Burnt are our homes
Ravaged and fled
Follow they would not dare.

Oh! Speed Bonny Boat like a bird on the wing
Onwards the sailors cried
Carry the lad that's born to be King
Over the sea to skye – e – e – e. ↗

This was sung by 20 of the class mates of the twins. A song of old
standing. The boys had loved this. They sang this continuously.
"Speed Bonny Boat" was known as their song.
The boys coffins marched by the mourners out of the
Porta-Cops home for the last time, while singing the above. The
congregation stood with stoic faces in wonderment. What had
really happened.

The Programs started this way.

1) The senior family members, along with the younger generations were placed as follows –

Lines were formed as they were taught –
   a) the males on the left hand side
   b) the girls and senior females were on the right hand side

Aunt V – Her strong alto was prevalent, she held her own.
Uncle Jobe – Blended with his base voice – in a very strong baritone – led the procession – to welcome the young ones on their journey.

1st Program –
The horses and carriages passed through the lined procession of elderly and new generations of family members.
The males of the families in strong baritone mixed with base – sang and blended with the elderly females and new generations of females.

Males	Females
zum zumie zum	Oh Sina dey
zumie zum zum zum	Rainey ah co co
zumie zum zumyum, zum, zum, zum, zum	Rainey ah co co, ah co, ah co
zumie zum zum zum	Rainey ah co co
zum zumie zum	Oh Sina dey
zumie zum, zum zum	Rainey ah co co

This ritual continued to the Porta-Cops house of residence and placed in the very large blue room. This was what Ms. Porta Cops' mother would have called "her Slavery death Quek, Quek."

This chanting was stopped when every thing was settled and placements were in order.

Mr. Porta Cops knew her boys knew and had drawn their own meaning to – "Oh Sina Dey." This was their meaning

Oh sina Dey's meaning –
We worked and toiled all the day long
Now we are tired and weary
As nights shadows have arrived.
Our work here has finished,
And now we are going all the way home.

Program #2
Made by Aunt Kathie – the familys' Poet/Song writer –
The service commenced at four o'clock. At three-thirty sharp everyone gathered on the Porta-Cops large ground, with the children in front to pay homage for the last time to the friends, relatives, nephews – of grand, greats so many times removed and all extended families

1) The marching procession #2 –
Headed by Reverent Joyce Marone
Known to the family by –
a) Cousin Joyce – younger – 1st generation family
b) Joycee
c) The Very Reverent
d) Pastor
e) The Very Reverent Joyce Marone – which was the correct way to address her.

The Very Reverent entered into the Blue room –
Commencement Exercises began –
Paying homage to the deceased –

Commencement Program #3
Time – 4 p.m.
Marching into the Blue Room –
Headed by The Very Reverend Dr. Joyce Marone

The Lords Prayer	singing rendition Auntie Kathie
Jesus Loves the Little Children	Ten younger friends
Lead me Gentle Home	Ten little cousins
Jesu, Joy of Man's Desiring	Sr. male members of family
The 23rd Psalm	Singing rendition – Aunt V
Oh Lovely Peace	Sr. female members of family
Obituary	Auntie Kathie
The 25th Proverb reading Verse 7	congregation
Sermon and Praise reading	The Very Reverend Dr. Joyce Marone
Speed Bonny Boat [Departure Song]	School children – 20
Closing Prayer	The Very Reverend Dr. Joyce Marone

Final Commencement Program #4
Time – 5 p.m.
To the Cemetery –
Back – Dam Cemetery 62 Courentyne Berbice, Guyana

A children affair –
1) children from school
2) neighbor's children
3) all the families' children

They marched in threes – [3] behind,
the horses and all the children followed singing
Aunt Kathie sang with the children.

The twins new home was their final resting place –
Song sang –
   a) We're marching to Zion
   b) Oh Sine dey
   c) This loss was told in songs, music, and verses

The twins were placed side by side – enbombed

There departure at entombment
Sang by Ms. Hilda –
   a) Oh Lovely peace
   b) Speed Bonny Boat like a bird on the wing

Complications at the ground the site of burial –
   a) Mom – grand – Ms. Hilda - Collapsed and was looked
       after by muscular Ian.
   b) At various times as the great aunts, aunts, and other
       family members all collapsed.
   c) The men of the family were there to support and comfort
       them, also lead them away.

We closed with love and peace.

We looked up towards the Heavens.
To see our little Birds Fly.
There they were gathering momentum.
We stood and looked, and looked, and looked
As they disappeared, we saw them no more.

Fly away!

you loving

Little birds.

The Porto-Cops Families

Thank you all for attending
You came and shared our pains
For that we are all grateful,
And now we must bid you adeu.

The Porta Cops families' thanks every one
For their togetherness, and being with us
For our – Songs of Pain.

Remember -   The boys stood on their burning decks.
                       Alone, but in togetherness.
                       Their battles were won,
                       Their flames were down,
                       They faced their fate head-on.

Thank you

The Families

Chapter 7

The Earls were the last ones to leave. Both daughters taking very heavy suitcases. Suddenly the suitcases jammed together and everything came out. Suitcase contents were flying everywhere. Out came the following –

1) Pure silver cutlery
2) The best crockery
3) Sheets
4) Fresh fruits including imported apples, and imported grapes
5) Jewelry
6) And some ready cash.

Great Nana said ' "Oh Elsie Earls you came with your family to grieve with us, and now you are leaving with my things in your cases." "Fie for shame."

Elsie Earls claimed she never knew how these things found there way into these cases. She did ask forgiveness saying –

Please, Oh Great Nana,
Spare me from this shame and disgrace
Forgive a weakened soul.
A soul that knows right from wrong,
With a spirit that is weak as water.

Please Great Nana
Forgive my sinful ways.
I know now my head and eyes are larger than my stomach.
There is greed and jealousy imbreded in me.
I am now trying to straighten my life,
And hope there will be forgiveness.

Elsie Earls directed her children to unpack what did not belong to them. The whole family did comply to this suggestion to Great Nana before finally departing.

Ms. Hilda Porta Cops tried settling into her now silently empty home.
She kept hearing different sounds that one would normally hear when it was quiet. Now these sounds were making her jumpy. She was now expecting to see the twins bouncing out of their rooms at any time. This was too much for Ms. Hilda to bear. She closed her eyes and said –

Please give me the strength to persevere
Believing that our destiny was all marked for us to bear
Lives were given, lives were taken away from us.
This grieving takes time and all one's energy.
My babies are gone, and I am left alone.
Now I am but a hallow shell without a heart
With emptyness enough to fill my mind.
Oh you of perfect peace be kind, and lean on me

With these few words she bent her head and broke into a flood of tears. Loud, pitiful, heart wrenching gut wrenching, soul searching tears. In fact this was the first time Ms. Hilda broke down and had a proper cry. She cried for their suddenly, quick, withdrawal from her.
She cried for all the wonderful times short years of togetherness and unity.
Dear Ms. Hilda could not stop her shower of tears. She then settled for the night and took on the restlessness of a troubled sleeper. A person flaying her limbs and body all over the bed, longing for some comfort but could not receive any.
This was a stressful time for her. By now her two babies would have brought an early morning breakfast with tea, fried eggs, fried

bread, butter and milk. Prior to helping her with her activities of daily living. Now she has to provide this service all by herself.

This was a week of colds. A kaleidoscope of colors and shapes. Some soothing, some brash, but the majority brought energy, sometimes bright lights, darkness, and dimness to Ms. Hilda. These were unforgettable times for Ms. Hilda Protacops. Her thought processes became disturbed. At times she was not aware of the changes of time; days, evenings, nights, it made no difference. They all rolled into one.

Ms. Hilda Porta-Cops become withdrawn and isolated. Her appetite began to dwindle. Her weight loss began to be noticeable. She had given up. Dear Ms. Hilda felt so alone. She kept complaining about hearing the children's voices.

She kept thinking about her children, their enclosement and cemented into the earth beneath. Also kept wondering and ruminating regarding –

1) Are they really down in the earth not moving, but decaying.

2) Is there really life after death; what would one reappear as. She was sure she saw some chest movement on one of her babies before she fainted.

3) What if they were not lifeless but alive and was given the embalming fluid.

4) Should I tell someone what I saw.

5) Am I going crazy. What is happening to me.

6) Would this be a repercussion of what had happened in Africa many years ago, when the buried relative sat up in the coffin. He was in a coma, and awoke. Of course there were no embalmment fluids in those days.

7) Did I as mother/grandmother did the correct thing. Ms. Hilda gave a big sigh and shuddered. They were locked away in that awful place beneath. Where everyone returns to in the end. With tears rolling down her cheeks dear Hilda placed her head into her hands, muttering, trying to hold back her tears –

I am losing my mind.
Please give me the purpose to go on,
So I can face all adversities.
I do need assistance and some understanding
To combat these demons of negativity

So forgive my wiltering mind.
Everyone is going away from me,
As I go into my mature years,
it appears that all things and relatives disappear,
leaving me empty and full of loneliness.

Dear Ms. Porta-Cops cried herself to sleep this night. and many
more lonely nights. That to her was the worse time. I never
knew one could acquire such fluids and tears, and not become
dehydrated, lonely Hilda said to herself.

Chapter 8

Dear Ms. Hilda sat reminiscing about the past two months. The last of her children whom have now departed to be with their biological parents. She was everywhere with her thoughts. She began thinking about customs, mannerisms, and the things that one does to suit nature habits. She knew that in Dutch Guyana, it took seven days of preparations before following the burial procession on the Saturday which would have become the eight day.

Suddenly Ms. Hilda started to leave the home with a zippered bag. No one knew what was in this large bag. She continued to be quiet, withdrawn, isolated, very poor appetite, eyes red, tear dried cheeks. She would never respond to any questions. Things got worst. Ms. Hilda started returning home in disarray. Her hair became an untidy mess. The family had a meeting and decided that this lovely lady must be followed.

She was found lying on the tomb of the twins, her small pillow under her head in the fetal position. There she would cry herself to sleep, well covered with her blanket.

It was a hard job to remove Ms. Hilda. Everyone tried talking to her, others praying, crying, and feeling the pain of Dear Ms. Hilda's grief, and loss. It was not until she dreamed about her mother who passed on years ago in Dutch Guyana, that Ms. Hilda stopped going there.

In this dream Ms. Hilda's mother told her not to keep coming to the graveside, crying continuously, as the neighbors are being disturbed. They are not receiving any rest, and would really like to catch up on that lost time. She was also plainly told that harm would befall her if this behaving continued.

Again there was a family meeting and it was agreed that their aunt could never be left on her own, and must be removed graciously to another area from the gravesite, thus making it impossible for their dear aunt to return there unescorted.

This was a family venture, even friends aided. This separation was the worst. In her present home, she came as a young bride with her husband. Her children all grew up and were married from her home. Her last two pumpkins grew up here. She, Ms. Hilda, was held in her husband's arms as they crossed the threshold on the first day in their new home.

Now everyone but herself were removed from this house of love in caskets.

This was a house of love, togetherness, happiness and oneness. Now it is a place of sadness, loneliness, despair, and depression.

With all these tangled thoughts jumping everywhere tears started to flow. She looked for her dear friend, her childhood of impishness – "Dear Ms. Daisy." They were friends from toddlers if one could really believe such a thing. They were still together after all these years. At times it was joked they both had two houses, throughout all the joy, sorrows and bitterness life had served them, they held each other steadfastly.

This was, the first major separation for these two sisters friends. They both lost their husbands, a few months a part. They were also great friends. These were losses on both sides. This bond was strong.

It was now time to part. No more reminiscing consistantly walking towards her niece Florence's car. Ms. Hilda turned to wave goodbye saying through tears, and trying to bite her lips to gain some control, whispered softly –

"Who is this that caused these pains,
and tore my heart to shreds.
The pain of these deep separations
Leaves one weak, lethargic and destroyed.
All that is needed now is to face my grief head on.

All my children have departed.
There is no one to wipe my brows.
I sit with sadness everyday,
Wondering what would happen to me now.
I was so sure they would put me away.
Now here am I all alone and sad.

Those whom I held most dear
Have now left my side.
Now I am standing all alone,
A female with no one.
About to start anew by herself.

As she drove away, the sound she was hearing from the car formed a tune like old times when she was with Daisy. She whispered sadly –
"Hop-Kin-de,
Dop-Kin-de
Oh; what you do to me
What you do to me
Oh; what you do to me
Hop-Kin-de
Dop-Kin-de
Oh, what you do to me
From the moment you're mine."

This brought her to the new home. Ms. Hilda was well known in her village. Everyone had already gathered at her gate awaiting her arrival. They all started clapping, singing and cheering in welcome. She received a greeting fit for a queen, as a queen she was.
The house was fixed to Ms. Hilda's wishes. Herthings were transferred over. At the door there was a large welcome sign, balloons, streamers, gospel music and lots to eat. The house was a gift from the younger generations. She was loved.

Speeches were made; the young were dancing with the hot rhythms of the reggie music. The great Bob Marley music took over the lawn with Ms. Hilda, or aunt, also Queen, as she was called. Her favorite "Buffalo soldier" was played that reminded her of some of her old time slavery songs, even the grands and great grands and other family members knew the song but never the meanings even though they could translate their songs in English.

The booming bongos were very hip tantalizing then came the favorites of the elderly in Ms. Hilda's and Daisy's era, the beats were great. Just to hear them say these words –

Oh Sina dey
Rainy a co-co;
Rainy a co-co-a-co-a-co,
Rainy a co-co.
Oh Sina dey
Rainy a co-co.

This they sang on any occasion when departing. According to Ms. Hilda she felt as if every one was there. She would sometimes say with even one singing in their different scales it brought tears to one's eyes.

To the younger ones those words meant –

"We worked and toiled all day long.
Now we are tired and weary,
And night's shadows has arrived.
Our work here was completed,
And we are going all the way home."

To these children that was the meaning of Ms. Hilda's "Oh! Sina dey."

This day will always stay fresh in one's memory.

This was good for a start over. It was a new beginning. It became the best of times for Ms. Hilda as she lifted her skirt in both hands and took her time doing a little of the highland fling. All in all good memories was the name of the new start that Ms. Hilda would take into her new home for a fresh start.

Ms. Hilda began to settle into her new accommodation. She felt stronger everyday.

Her thoughts came on the past and her dear daddy. He was a man of culture, courage, and much love. Very distinguished. She could not understand how two countries so near be so far apart in customs. In her father's country in the British section of Guyana, her father the son of one of the head slaves was from a large family. He himself had a large family of sons, and Ms. Hilda. When he died, he was kept in a corner of the home in his bedroom. He had passed away in his house in the country area.

Ms. Hilda remembered seeing her father –

1) Lying on a steele bed a little larger than his this steele bed had four legs at the legs were four buckets very large. Between these legs were two large basins, with mats under them.

On the top of this steele bed was her father's body surrounded with ice chipped in various pieces, and replaced continuously. There were holes on the steele bed that led into the buckets and basins on the floor. These also were emptied frequently by designated family members and male friends. there were no embalming in those days in this third world country, especially in her district. The villagers were very supportive.

The villagers made all the manual preparations for example –

1) an area were prepared for the burial
   a) the chosen site
   b) the cement for the first beginning of the family plot
   c) the casket was made with a lovely glass over grey, and white linen to line the inside of the casket. A little glass flap with a see through cover stating her father's - age, date of birth, and time of his demise.

2) They were delegated to various tasks – for example
   a) cooking
   b) sewing
   c) various positions of helping

The village mother – the oldest female in the village came to assist with a few selected villagers and family members, also participated with their knowledge in the burial processes.

This was a solemn affair when everything was completed the male villagers all assisted in placing the deceased into his casket, only in those days the word used was coffin."

Fare-Well Party for Ms. Hilda
Down Yonder green valley

The Ash Grove –

Down yonder green valley where streamlets meander
When twilight is fading, I pensively rove,
Or at the bright moontide in solitude wander
Amid the dark shades of the lonely Ash grove.

'Twas there while the blackbird was joyfully singing
I first met my dear one, the joy of my heart;
Around us for gladness the bluebells were ringing
Ah! then little thought I how soon we should part.

Still grows the bright sunshine o'er valley and mountain
Still warbles the blackbird his note from the tree;
Still trembles the moonbeam on steamlet and fountain,
But what are the beauties of nature to me.

With sorrow, deep sorrow, my bosom is laden
All day I go mourning in search of my love.
Ye echoes, O tell me, where is the sweet maiden?
She sleeps 'neath the green turf down by the Ash grove.

Traveling – but very scared.
Captain, Captainn, put me ashore↗
I don't want to go anymore↘
Itaname gwan frighten me↘
Itaname gwan hut me belly↘

CHORUS: La, la, la, la   →   *Gwan frighten me*
                 La, la, la, la   →   Oh hut me belly
                 La, la, la, la   →   Don't go any moe
                 La, la, la, la   →   Oh put me ashore

La, la, la ,la – oh – ha, la, la, la.
Hut me belly – oh – Hut me belly
Ga anymoe – Na – ga anymoe
Fughten me – gwan – frighten me
Put me ashore – yea – Put me ashore.

Itaname gwan frighten me↗
Itaname, oh itanami, itanami gwan hurt me belly
Oh itaname, oh itanami, oh itaname ↗
Itaname, i-ta-na-me, i-ta-na-me, I—ta—na--me

Poems of love for Ms. Hilda
Oh! We really love you

Yes! Oh mother of love.
We love you for your gentleness.
Your giving nature is well known
Indeed! You have the world at your feet.

That one could be so gentle.
Giving so much comfort,
loving their neighbors, and welcoming them,
As you welcomed with love your family.

Your kindness knew no bounds.
We will always remember you dear Mother.
Oh! You really are a mother
Everyone's mother of love.

> From the neighborhood,
> With Lots of Love

Poems of love for Ms. Hilda — to welcome her.

Your Gift

Yes mother of many welcome to you.
Now you have received more gifts,
and these must be gifts of love,
feelings, supports, and carings.

You will never be alone my dear.
As you are filled with lots of sharing.
Now we all would be saving for you.
Our lives, generosities, and givings a plenty.

So our dear Mother, grandmother,
And to many, sisters to the elders.
We will always be by your side,
Whether you want us to or not.

From the Grove's Family
We'll always love you

Party for Ms. Hilda –

Satyra Girl

One day I went to the back dam,
And I see Satyra lay don dey.
I asked Satyra wa shea do dey
Satyra lift up she clothes
and wine like a Buxton Bull

Oh Satyra mo man deh
Oh Satyra mo man deh
Yes Satyra mo man deh
Oh Satyra mo man deh
Yes Satyra mo man deh
Yes Satyra mo man deh
Yes Satyra mo man deh
Oh Satyra mo m—an d—eh.

They flounced, skirts held in their hands, legs and boots kicked
back. Oh this celebration was loud.
There were clapping, singing, tramping with hands in the air. This
was a grand time for all. These senior girls could really do a gig.

Leaving the Farewell Party – Song by Ms. Hilda

I trust in God.
where others help had failed.
On mountain tops
or on the glassie seas.
Though billows roll
he leads my soul.
My heavenly father watches over me.

I trust God.
I know he'll care for me.
On mountain tops
or on the glassie seas
Though willows roll
He'll watch my soul,
My heavenly father watches over me.

Singing lusterly she burst into tears as she waved her hands, blew
kisses and hugs, while she made her departure.

Chapter 9

Strange how times have changed. 1) Now there are funeral homes (2) Churches, 3) In the house which was the front room, or the sitting room there were spaces under the house or yard as these were called. After services were over the family's as well as the villagers would march to the cemetery for the burial of their loved ones. There was also a service, as this was the final resting place for the departed.

Everyone goes back to their homes at the end of the parting. At the night of the ninth day after the death all spent a quiet day, and the mother, wife, or kin of the deceased would spend that day at the cemetery, planting flowers, talking, writing, and leaving messages. Also at times some family members mark their surroundings, so that area would be well known.

At certain times for example –

1) Birthdays
2) Special holidays
3) Anniversaries to the year or years of passing, family members will visit. They would also keep the area clean, white wash the tombs, place flags and at times an everlasting light at the deceased foot area.

Things have certainly changed for the better. Shaking her head, eyes swollen from crying. She appeared to be weeping continuously these days and could not even control those showers sighing she said in a timid voice –

Please give me the strength to persevere.
Help me to curb my grief and accept my loss.
We are only here for a short while.
Please, no more sadness, or heartache,
In my state of deep depression

I hope that this sadness would come to pass,
Bringing a bright new star in its wake.

Ms. Hilda continued with her thoughts. Muttering about all her children and grandchildren's passings and the time changes that has passed between everyone's death.

"Oh goodness," she said. I am still alive to witness these changes, also the new present. My children went into the country's mortuary. Their post mortem was performed there, prior to being brought home and placed into her sitting room for the days services and preparations, before their burials. Everything went smoothly. Now my babies are at peace with their biological parents who had proceeded them years ago.

Her wondering searches continued. Ms. Hilda a strong believer of reincarnation, started to imagine into whose spirits her babies would return as. Naming, and placing her priorities in this reincarnation processes. She had –

1) A new born who in due time might be acting as one of her babies

2) A loving new pet – a dog – with human understanding

3) A young toddler with old ways for her age – or his age
   Reminding her of a loved one that has passed on years ago With her thoughts of life after death or her frequent visits to the cemetery, dear Ms. Hilda would imagine her children by the entrance of their new homes waving in greetings and welcome. She felt their presence very close to her, and knew it was the families that had passed on. Happy in her belief she thanked them for looking after the new arrivals, her babies, all being in togetherness as she had taught them. She was preparing to leave Ms. Hilda said while gathering her belongings –

goodbye my children you are at peace now.
Look after each other in your world.
I do not know when we would meet,
but rest assure we would.

Walking away from her departed family, she continued –

I was blessed my dear babies, when I received you both.
It was a good time, a time of peace and joy.
I now know where you would always be.
So goodbye my loves; goodbye my families.
You came in peace, and have departed with peace,
Peace, Peace, be still.

Ms. Hilda was aware that the grieving process takes about one year. It was almost that time, but still her heart felt very heavy. Her tears continued to pour at the least sound, word, or aggravation. Sleeping was very hard. She was very isolative, which seemed to be her form of imprisonment, as she had cut herself away from society. Ms. Hilda became weak, had marked weight loss, listlessness, lethargy and non-communicative. The neighbors watched her for one day, after finding Ms. Hilda sitting in the same position for the whole morning. They did not know what time she was sitting outside, and for how long. It was questionable the amount of hours Ms. Hilda kept in one place, or rooted to one area.

The neighbor's called her family, who in turn notified other family members, police, and an ambulance. Ms. Hilda just sat whimpering, tremulously, her frail figure just racked continuously in tears that soaked the front of her dress.

She was transferred to the local hospital, where she was admitted via the psychiatric unit from the psychiatric emergency room for severe depression with catatonia state. She was placed on (24) twenty four hours close observations. She was also placed on suicidal observations. Ms. Hilda's families were all very supportive. They all attended every meeting, and did whatever it took to help their frail aging Queen.

Ms. Hilda's condition improved. Slowly she gained weight, began conversing. Her eye contact was very positive. Her interaction with other patient peers was positive. She verbalized her needs to anyone who would listen.

By the time for discharge Ms. Hilda was positive in her appearances. She could also perform all her activities of daily living. Her lovely cheeks was very soft and smooth. She was her old self again.

In the end Ms. Hilda was discharged to a family member, where she would be living. Her belongings were already transported.

She was very lucky, as she was accepted into a day program. This made Ms. Hilda very excited. Her follow up care appointment was made. There was a surprised farewell party prior to her departure the night before by the other patients and staff.

Chapter 10

Thinking about her ancestors before her. As a child both her good friend Ms. Darsy and her used to laugh their heads off at the way these senior family members looked, Ms. Darsy mused. Now here they are dressing the same way, following customs, acting as these passed seniors did years ago, and have that strong altone voice that was passed down the line.

She still remembers the areas and their habits – For example
1) In the country areas –
   a) Good-in-tent – These are very strong creole areas. Very strong "ochu" families and background.
   Families in these areas are very clanish, heavily altone voices; very rich voices in singing along with high sopranos, bass, a very good blend. Lots of stories about life after death, as they say – "the passing" or one could hear them saying – "Was the circle broken," tales about the open cemetery burial sight. These folk finds strength in togetherness.
   b) Essequibo – Family members which are very large in numbers – go out of their way to welcome visitors. They would generally close ranks in a minute against any stranger or strangers, members of the villages, if at anytime they feel threatened. They also form clusters. They are really a very happy family bunch of villagers.
   c) Berbice/New Amsterdam/Courentyne.

The vast range of families in all of these areas are very clannish. They would close ranks immediately at any sign of danger, sickness, death, or irritability. They form large groups, and never accept any strangers. There was a story that explains what I mean claims Ms. Hilda. One of the great great aunt's had passed away suddenly.

In those days the demise was kept in a back room on an ice-tray as long and larger than the deceased. Large pieces of ice were placed on and around the deceased, with buckets on all four points to receive the water drips. This was a very large family. It was said that great, great, great grand Papa had twenty four sons legally with his wife – who was very small in stature and came from the Congo; a small slip of a girl "Papa" got his daughters from outside of the marriage, with various other females – just as many female children as the twenty four males. The family claimed that "Papa" was preparing to go back to his country in Africa prior to his passing. I vaguely remember what was done with his remains. During the nights of mourning and the day of his burial, the large gathering consisted of the following –

There were/are four corners in a room, with a middle divided into –

1) The Chinese side of the family in one area/corner.
2) The Portuguese side of the family in another area/corner.
3) The Ameridgenese Indians/and other Indians in the family in another area/corner – those with mixed parentage
4) The Negroes – as was called in those days was in another corner/area.
5) In the middle the Indians in the family would be situated between all of these, visitors usually mingle with everyone. All the children usually play together in good spirits and with happiness regardless.

It was always said whenever there is a family function, and outsiders are invited, this would have to be kept outside in a big hall, or there would be no room for outsiders. Families tend to be very clustered with no outsiders.

Those families before the Berbice River are superficial in all areas. They are also very class conscious.

In New Amsterdam – our families there were also stubborn and rude. They do not welcome strangers immediately. They usually take time to know someone prior to acceptance. They are also very heavy into class consciousness, could be snobbish, and have stronger ties with Surinam.

6) The Capital – Our relatives there are completely indifferent. Their mannerisms are superstitious, suspicious and could be selfish at times. They are completely different from other country areas. Their mother play an important part in their lives. Some of their children are also stubborn. Should not be trusted by outsiders.

Ministers from larger countries, with any available histories not noted come to open churches, and have meetings. Some stay for years, or short visits which would be weeks, months before departing the country.

Chapter 11

There is a strong influence of Creole Clusters. I do say that by the way they presented themselves for example –

1) They form little groups in their togetherness, dressing in their African attire –
    a) Flowered colored dresses, with head scarves to match their dresses and sometimes broad hats over these scarves to protect them from the hundred degree temperatures.
2) These lovely colored dresses were comprised of sunflowers,
3) Calypso colored dresses.
4) Multi-colored dresses.
5) Bland colors
6) Cotton, silk, rice bags – cottons in brown, flour bags whites well bleached with limes, lemons, and salt.
7) Cloths with patterns of daisies; roses, buttercups, hibiscus, along with many more lovely designs of flowers. Some insisted on having very large pockets below their waists, for everything to be placed for safekeeping. Some of these dresses also have small laced pockets around the left breast pockets. These grand dressers made the dresses their daily attire. Only now I could understand the importance of these gestures, their fashion statements, their appearances of yesteryear.
1) They do have dress up Sundays for –
    a) Churches
    b) Important functions with a great yen for Creole stories where everyone gathers exchanging stories of old times and other tales from years ago. These given gifts of talking, with facial expressions that holds

ones attention during the understanding of these tales. Smiling at the way things have a way of turning full circle, with the past seems to be staring right in front of her and Ms. Daisy's faces. Ms. Hilda remembers the best time for these stories, good situation areas like –

1) The country areas in all the coasts. In Ms. Hilda's days there were no street lights in the country areas – that was the correct medium for our Creole stories.

Years ago during slavery there were times that you will hear or see images from those era, again in sharp continance, always with their heads tied in the females, and special hats for the men's head. Even the cemetery, with the trees being planted in those areas reminded Ms. Hilda of her past, the chilly feelings she always felt in her bones with the thought passing by one of those places. Just the idea of being sealed into something that was made of cement/concrete. What would have happened if she had not really passed on. She knew no one would really hear her even if she screamed her poor old head off. Even so having tons upon tons of earth placed on top of her, then mashed down along with water pouring on top of that would make the earth soft. These people really wanted to make sure there was no way to escape. Everything frightened her. The thought of being left alone forever. Poor Ms. Hilda had to close her eyes and groan at where her thinking processes was taking her.

Chapter 12

Rethinking her Dutch ancestorship Ms. Hilda Porta-Cops vaguely remembers her own mother's passing many years ago. She was about fourteen years old, and an only child for her mother, also the only girl for her father. She knew as the only closest relative alive for her mother certain things had to be carried out/performed after her mother's demise. She could never tell her relatives about that part. She had made that promise to her mother long before she had passed away. In that Dutch society one do not share that kind of information. No one really wanted to press her to reveal such things that would make her feel uncomfortable and reluctant to share. For her babies she kept some of her customs that were performed privately, between her and the babies along with Aunt Vetty. These two were the only seniors alive in the family, and of course best friend everlasting Daisy – Ms. Daisy, or otherwise called "the sisters," that would be Ms. Hilda and Daisy who were both of the young ages of eighty-two years.

No one asked questions. We all knew it was hush-hush. We honored her that much and therefore granted her request not to pry. As usual she came out busting in phrases –

Promises! Promises! Promises
Are you making me promises to keep.
- or – making some that could be broken.
A promise given is one to keep
It signifies trust, togetherness, and unity.
This promise that I have
gives a lifetime of strength, trustworthiness,
And a mind of less stress, heartache, and tears.
We must keep our promises.

With a whimsical smile she continued with her reminiscings thinking about her dreams laced with premonition that usually comes to pass. What kind of gifts are these. She remembers early the day of the accident when her children had passed away.

She awoke early that morning and a deep cloud hung over her head. Tired as she would it just could not this cloud stood and stuck in one position. She remembered how she had lost her appetite, and just knew something dreadful was going to happen. She felt her soul leaving her body, her will power was fading. She clasp her hands together, streams of tears pouring down her cheeks she whispered –

What is going to happen today. Oh Master!
What sadness are we to expect this day.
Please support and strengthen us to face whatever would be our fate.
I am scared of the unknown, and so too is everyone
Give us the strength please save our children.
Take me instead this exchange would be fair.

Ms. Hilda continued crying. She could not tell which one of her grands were going, or if it was another family member that she would be able to deal with. Only being selfish she wanted all her babies alive. She wanted to be the one to depart if something was to happen. This time she said quietly, slowly with eyes shut tightly, lips bleeding where she had held them with her teeth to prevent the tears from flowing said –

Not my babies, not my babies; No! my babies.
Oh NO! Never the babies, Never my babies,
Do not suffer them, nor take them away.
I know someone is departing today
Only, please; Just not the babies
Never; Never; Never; Our Babies.

Everything was coming back as if it was yesterday. It was over three years at this time since her babies had departed, yet everything felt as if it just happened. She felt like tearing her heart out, and also hoped no other family children pass away before her time comes. This kind of grief never goes away. No one would want to bury their babies before them.

Ms. Hilda did not want to be called judgmental. It was not the way someone goes away. It was not normal to lose one babies like that. She broke with a hic-cough, shook her head and murmured:

My daughter's children who were now mine,
Were taken away from me you see.
My daughter's children who were now mine.
Went and left me behind.

It was I who should have gone and leave them behind. They were strong, young, and had a promising future. They were my babies, my daughter's children, you see. Now they are no more, and I am all alone.

Lying in bed after her nightly snack dear Ms. Hilda had a flash back about life in her Dutch country. She had missed her husband then, and now she missed him more than ever. She just wanted to be with him and the babies, also her other family members and friends. All she was ready for was to pass over to see and be with her pumpkins. There was –
1) No one to chat with
2) No one to visit
3) She just did not have the strength to continue anymore

Poor Ms. Hilda felt so alone,
1) Isolated.
2) And at times became tangential, her mind going here, there and everywhere.

3) No one to pass pleasantries.
4) Sometimes her sentences might hardly make sense, but from the bits and pieces that one hears her say, everyone knows its about her last two babies and her husband.

It was true a mother's love would never go, whether the children are here or not.

Ms. Hilda Porta-Cops after various family meetings, refused to stay with her nieces, insisting on staying alone with her past, thoughts, and fresh memories until her time had come. Trying to see the level of her confusion, Ms. Hilda's age was brought up in conversation, naturally according to Ms. Hilda, the twins knew and that was all that matters, and freshly added "So there" the family members all said together. You cannot help loving our young aunt.

As a Dutch the other family members were prepared to take Ms. Hilda back home should she desire that. She had instructed the twins, being sure she would have passed away before her babies – or – so she thought. It was a good thing those two had decided to share this secret with other family members before their departure, for now Ms. Hilda was not talking – or – choose not to respond to any one.

Gone was all connection to Dutch Guyana, their customs, and other senior members who had passed on in her country.

She really wanted to be with her babies. Knew they were waiting for her, hence her hurry to be with them.

Calmly and in a soft voice, this darling said –

A hurry; A hurry, A hurry, I'll always be.
My two pumpkins have left me.
Now it's my turn to be with them.
I'll not be kept back for anyone.
It is my time to go.

Of course we all knew Dear Hilda as we now called her, refused to leave her detached residence. Her faint excuse; her children would not know where to find her. She did not want to miss them. Everyone tried various angles to no avail.

The decision was, the family will take turns to care in every way for our "Dear Hilda.

Chapter 13

The family took turns monthly staying with Dear Hilda. It was working out well. Although objectionable everyone cherished her with lots of love and nourishment.

Dear Hilda whenever she wants to go on a reminiscing journey would pretend to be asleep. These were be coming very frequent. Dear Hilda really believed those journeys would bring her closer to her goal, that was being with her children and husband.

This started her thinking of her husband and his tragic disappearance. With a deep sigh, she realized that losses and sadness had followed her from one Guyana to the next. Same last name, but different cultures. One Dutch speaking the other English speaking.

Her husband, dear Will as he was called, went over to the English speaking Guyana and never came back. He was reported lost in the interior. This happened many years ago, and this time Dear Will was very heavy in Ms. Hilda/Dear Hilda's thoughts.

Was he lost in the jungles of Guyana, murdered or went away with a female. Did he have any other children. When questioned Dear Hilda really believed her husband was alive, but did not want to be found. She cried frequently at these times, and would even call out his name. All these years she kept hoping he would return sometime and be with her again. She had kept her thoughts all these years to herself when he did not return home to their country, after he was reported missing in British Guyana.

She removed to the harbor of Surenam/Dutch Guyana. After spending a year waiting and hoping for news of her husband, Ms. Hilda decided to move over to British Guyana, so as to be nearer when he was found. She came over with all their belongings, along with their children's. Years later he was declared deceased without evidence of a body.

There was nothing Ms. Hilda could have done. She had to continue with her life, and provided a father and mother for her now fatherless children, even though she believed he would one day reappear.

Wishing she had placed her feet firmly on the ground, when the discussion started for her Dear Will to travel to her new country for work, she knew he would be still with her, being happy together with their children. Now she had aged and grown up in a foreign country, speaking a foreign tongue, learning a foreign language, making that country her home. So here she was knowing any time she would depart and be buried on foreign soil, where her customs were very much different from theirs. She now realized her wishes could never be carried out for her, after her demise, groaning she said –

I would not leave you my dear children.
I would never leave your side.
I the great matriarch of the family,
the mother for all of you.
Together we came, together we would remain,
And all in unity we would remain.

To her husband this loving brave lady said –

The day we were joined it was for life.
The vows we made it stayed with us
Even though we are apart
Your memories lingers on
Please collect me by our meeting place,
And together we would walk,
Hands clasped we meet our destination in unity.

After her mutterings Ms. Hilda had her usual catnap. This time she had a longer nap. Either before or after meals Ms. Hilda insisted on her naps that she receive so she could travel, and continue with her tangental musings that played such an important part in her fixed life. This time her thoughts were on herself, remembering that she came to her adopted country with nothing. She had left her home with only her children and clothing. Her good job, as she was a Deputy Principal in her country. She was a very educated young lady, and saw to it that her children were educated in every way.

In this new country, she had to learn new habits, phrases, customs, and paid much attention to her English pronunciations.

Ms. Hilda continued her education in her new country, and was also promoted as Deputy Principal of one of the largest Roman Catholic schools in the country, until she retired and went over to her son's Private School which was very famous, and had a reputation for producing very brilliant scholars she was also Head Mistress of her son's Middle School.

Dear Hilda started off as a seamstress while studying. A great adoptor and bilingual she was an asset to her new place of living. She maintained her same standards of existence as she was doing in her native land. With a pleasant smile about her inner thoughts and herself she said –

I knew I was all alone
Me; a single mother, trying to make ends meet.
Received the perseverance and persistance
That all single mothers seems to receive.

The power to face all new matters daily
Bright faces to be welcomed
The neighborhood support and greetings system
Was a welcome gift of new friends to greet you

It was a good decision that was made jointly by all. To this day there still were no regrets. As she felt his presence with her continuously she never felt alone until now as she was weak and melancholy from all of her tragedies.

Her spirits were low. Her immune system was not up to par, so she became a lonely medium for infections. This was being monitored by everyone.

Dear Hilda was so grateful for all the attention and care she was receiving. There were some good days, and at times her thoughts and feelings were down to zero. Along with a few arthritic pains and shortness of breath, Dear Hilda was doing quite well. She remained quite alert thus all her past thinking were more painful than others, who were not so gifted. The only insistence being Dear Hilda's urge to leave this world. This she plainly insisted on. The Idea of being left alone as others have departed was very frightening for her. One evening after a loud clap of thunder Dear Hilda sat upright and said in a voice filled with fear –

No! Never alone, never alone my dear.
What would become of me dear friends.
Why me, without a future and alone.
Please do not leave me alone.
Promise to remove me before the others have left.
Please, Please, not ever alone,
You promised never to leave me alone.

Chapter 14

Everyone realized Dear Hilda was seeing her past floating before her. With her memory Dear Hilda remembered it all. She spoke about –

1) Her beautiful lovely mother who was a black skinned tall refined woman of color. She also had long black shoulder length hair which was very curly. Her teeth was lily white, very long eye lashes, jet black and eye-brows well shaped, this was a trade mark from the family.

Indeed Ms. Hilda always boasted about her lovely parent who was frequently called "Black Beauty," the love of every male, and the most hated by the female. She was a treasure to behold this tall Athletic Queen, who was a strong descendent from the transportation of slaves to her country. "The Dutch Guyana," smilingly she said to herself

My mother, My sister,
Your memories lingers on
You have left, but it still feels like yesterday
I am on my journey, a very long one.
But I will be with you dear Mother.
Just as soon as my travels are over.

So please abide dear Mother by me.
Your wait is almost over.
You do have the patience of Jobe,
With love shared and kisses aplenty.
Now abide with me dear mom,
For the evenings tide would soon be here.

In between her remanisings and wondering, this dear lady would mutter at times "come children." We then realize she was teaching the children either a dancing step, a singing tenor voice training or even a play's verse. Ms. Hilda was a well known choreographer for her countries, and trained many children in various plays and exercises. This gift she passed on to one of her daughters, who also became a teacher for a very prestigious high school in her adopted country. This daughter, an outward show for distinction was loved by everyone for her play abilities and all the other gifts she had acquired at Ms. Hilda's hand. The president of her adopted country even thanked her for her many services she had performed and taught the residents of her new country.

This daughter was well gifted, traveling all over her new country, teaching in various schools exercises in culture, dancing and singing. After retiring from public life she became an ordained minister at one of the "Zion" churches in the country. She was then given the title of "Reverent." Make no mistake this daughter took her ministry seriously. Proudly she looked up as if seeing her daughter's faces, and with an impish grin, her little chin raised pronouncedly in the air with its little dimple said –

My daughters you have done very well for yourselves.
Such strength, knowledge, and understanding.
So much togetherness, oneness and bonding
Makes me very proud to be your Mother.

To know me, a single parent have produced such genuis. All qualified, giving back to the country
In gratitude for what it has done for you.
I am proud of you my children.
For what you have completed before you departed.
So peace my children, peace with my love.

I know not whose image we would return as
But know this, we will all meet,
Never mind the forms we would take,
Remember I am on my way, so hold my space.

Dear Hilda knows she will be leaving this world a proud, pleased and satisfied parent for all children, adopted children, grand children, and great, great grand children. What a successful accomplishment I have received for all my struggles. Ms. Hilda said quietly. Also knowing she would continue to expect from the new generation, all that she had requested their parents to pass on to the next generation, and those to follow. She knew at any time she would be ready to depart. Ms. Hilda asked forgiveness of her mother for not joining her in Surinam the capital of Dutch Guyana as was planned years ago. She has her family with her, and her last grand children's/children. She needed to be among her babies, so her soul could be at peace.

Ms. Hilda Porta-Cops was sinking fast. She made plans for her burial –

1) Hymns to sing –   a) Thy will be done.
                       b) The Lord's Prayer.

2) Requested that the children carry on the service at her demise.

3) She did not want her customs from her country carried out. Her babies were the last

4) All her belongings must be shared by everyone. Placing her pastor to be in charge of making arrangements re-her demise.

5) Calling everyone and thanking them for their support throughout her milestones.

6) She had her funeral clothing, and everything was paid for. There was nothing for anyone to do but carry out all of her wishes. She gently kissed each of them, wishing them continued health, then she said –

Read the poem "Little Jim" it will tell you how I feel. Her favorite words of this was –
"He smiled to thank her as he took
Three tiny little sips."
"Mother the angels do so smile

And beckoned little Jim.

She then said all –

I have to go, I am being waited on,
She held the pastor's hands and whispered to him

Please see me to the gates and let me go.
Goodbye my families till we meet again.
I do love you all, and my work here is over.
I am now going for a rest.
I now need Peace perfect Peace.
Because the love of my father gentle leads me home.

Ms. Hilda Porta-Cops bid everyone one fare-well. The very close
relatives gather to leave. She was looking exceptionally bright
today. Very chatty, witty, and very peaceful until she went to
sleep.

Dear Hilda was a good sleeper. In the morning at six o'clock
when she was awakened by a longstanding family friend for her
early morning tea there was no response. Turning on the light
realized that dearest Hilda had passed away quietly in her sleep.
The perfect peace that she had always spoke about, she had
received while asleep in bed. In a state of shock, everyone joined
together saying –

You dear strong lady of class and courage.
You are now with past loved ones as you wanted.
We will miss your kindness and your flair.
A lady with a full heart of love, peace, and charity.
May you cross without any fear,
Just go with peace, peace within.

All of her wishes were granted. She was buried in the family's plot
near her last two babies. This was only fitting as it was the shock

of their passing that brought this end. Ms. Hilda Porta-Cops lived a life of a Gentle Queen and passed away with a Queen's Dignity. She was smiling gently as she was taken home. One could just picture her saying –

Thank you for granting my wish.
I have asked you to lead me home.
You have prevented me from falling on the wayside,
So now I have attained my goal.
For I was led gently home.

To this day the police never found out who killed the Port-Cops children. Ms. Hilda was much loved by everyone. She was a mother of many a friend for all, and a confidant for those who needed her.

Aunt V whispered something that only she knew what it meant. Also the loving deceased Ms. Hilda if she was alive. As Ms. Hilda was placed in the family's vault, Aunt V waving her hands into the air said in a strange high pitched voice –
Oh ju ma oh,
Oh ju ma oh,
Oh ju ma ma, oh oh Ke-Co
Kere lire ka oh
Oh ju ma ma, oh oh Ke-co
Kere lire ka oh
Oh na ce, oh ne, oh le-le.
Oh ne oh le-le quek key me----

Aunt V never finished. She stopped and whispered quietly "go in peace."

No one has ever dared to ask her what these words ever meant. Knowing Aunt V she would brush us off with something off the bean. Aunt then realized she was the last of the generation. She also must be the one with these final secrets.

Now was a new time; a new beginning, and the start of the next generation. The third generations of the new family.

Tragedy in a third World Country.
The Songs of Pain

The Last Will and Testament of Hilda Porta-Cops.

I Hilda Porta-Cops have left –

1) My Jewelry for the girls in our families – there are enough for all
2) The lands for all the male family members to be shared evenly
3) The houses to Aunt V to do whatever she wants, a business interests, monies,
4) All my clothes, memories, and whatever else she wants, to my Dear Friend, and Sister of naughtiness "Ms. Daisy" also Ms. Daisy to be buried with our family.
5) My monies to be shared to All my Families with $100,000, going to the church.
6) Please keep the peace and stay as sweet as you all are.
7) All my Helpers, Doctors, and nurses would be given a thank you by Aunt V.

Much love – to you all.
From – Hilda Porta Cops.

Witnessed by – Aunt Vetty [V]
Relationship – Sister of Ms. Hilda Port-Cops

Signed –   Attorney Selsein Hounds.
                Attorney – Selsein Hounds.

The Afterwards –
1) Everyone returned to the house to settle and eat light refreshments
2) Packing for their pending departure.
3) Some cleaning and staying over for a few days, then departures were quiet and uneventful.

At the reading of the will –
1) Aunt Pounce, Aunt Lonny, and Aunt Dejoyce, became angry as their names were not particularly mentioned, even though they were receiving gifts from the now deceased Ms. Hilda.

They took back all their gifts they had given Ms. Hilda during the past years. They made very long lists. There were a lot of tears, expressed anger, and bitterness.

The train ride back was quiet. This was completely different from the ride up.

Aunt Emma did say, she think whatever Ms. Hilda had left behind only the family members should take. Sister Yvette said – I can't stand these distant families, they try taking everything, and claim how close they were with the dead.

The other relatives stayed in their own corner until it was departure time on the ninth day and night.

Very close relatives and friends gather at the cemetery for prayers for those who stayed at home on the funeral day.

The morning continued for a year up to the anniversary of the departed. Everyone gathered together at this time. From that day the families tried getting on with their lives.

x x x x x x x x x

Ms. Hilda never found out who it was that pushed her children off the road into that vast amount of water, and drove off thus causing their deaths.

The case file was still in the open file for unsolved deaths years later.

The family plots in Dutch Guyana and British Guyana now called the Guyana Republic were maintained privately by some men the family hired in both countries. Everything was paid for indefinately.

Flowers were placed yearly.

Tombs were white washed every two years, and touched up whenever the caretakers felt the need.

Chapter 15

This younger generation of Porta-Cops decided that they should continue with their strong background of tribal customs and drums. There you could hear the beats of the bongoes, voices of all descriptions with the famous "Queh, Queh" songs at the Brides Wedding eves. For example –

1) Oh Janey Girl
   A wah da deh
   A me libing
   Oh he big an strong
   A me libing
   Oh ya use vasalene
   A me libing
   A me libing
   Yes ma libing

2) Oh, gal, ya masta a calling,
   Run come ga, run come ga.
   Oh gal, the big stick a coming,
   Run com ga, run com ga
   Ga, ga, ga, yea ga with him, yea ga with him
   Ga, ga, ga yea, ga with him, ga with him.

These villagers were always there for each celebrations. Dressed in their clothes of yesteryear, tying their bellies as they say with large knots of African materials, feet with shoes and socks, sneakers and socks, slippers and socks, also yatching and socks heads tied with materials to match waist-lines, footwears, dresses, or lovely hats.

Our people in those days would show the world their lovely silks, satins, expensive cottons, and jewelries. They dressed like Kings and Queens, and always carried their countries colors, habits, and tribal customs. They were all very proud people, and these things have now passed down to their new generation, and would be followed through to the next generations.

Then comes the pregnancies and babies' arrivals. You would then hear on babies arrival songs or Queh Queh for births, stampings and jubilations.

1) Come get the castor oil
   Ah ha, ah ha
   Do take the castor oil
   Ah ha, ah ha
   Then tie down ya belly
   Ah ha, ah ha
   Baby here, baby here
   Oh yes, oh yes.

This was my favorite –

Oh Lord,
A new chile a coming,
Weh de man deh, weh de man de
Fa he them sey he de fada.
Weh de man deh, weh de man deh.

Oh Lord,
The new chile he, a here now.
Show de man he, show de man he.
For he him sey he a de fada.
Mek him see him, mek him see him

Yes Lord,
Him see a him new pickney.
Look the fada, Look the fada,

Holding him new pick a-nee-nee
Thats the man deh, thats the man deh.

After all the different milestones, and by this time with training
in speeches, agilities gaits, and educations. Our people placed
themselves slowly but surely into the mainstream of societies,
climbing the career ladder with much fighting for secured places,
victimazations, open distructions even though Queen Victoria
had promised that we as a British colony would never be slaves
again. We fought for what we now have, and are still fighting for
more honest liberations.
The greatest song I truly believed was

  1) Oh sina dey
      Rainey ah co co.
      Rainey ah co co, ah co, ah co
      Rainey ah co co
      Oh sina dey
      Rainey ah co co.

The song for everything including the crossing over.
May this generation and all the future generations, live in peace,
unity, and togetherness; keeping in tune with all the past customs,
and histories of our generations.

Chapter 16

Dear Ms. Hilda Porta-Cops, well known as –

a) Ms. Hilda
b) Hilda
c) Mother Porta Cops
d) Mother
e) Granny
f) Cuz

She was a very religious individual, and came from very large families, with different customs due to their strict back-ground of direct African descendants of slavery
She was a third generation from slavery with connections from–

1) Libera
2) Cameroon
3) Congo
4) Parts of Nigeria

Ms. Porta-Cops along with other family members are really proud of their descendants, customs, and concentrated in teaching the next generations in songs and dances about their past. Ms. Hilda originated from Dutch Guyana, the capitol of which was Surinam.
Ms. Hilda was –

a) charming
b) up straight
c) elegant
d) brilliant female who always had her hands out in welcome mode for anyone who would like to stay at her dwelling for –
a) one night
b) multiple nights – or –

c)   as long as they wanted to stay at her dwelling

There were no limitations, and Ms. Hilda would always say yes, even if all the rooms were packed. No one was never turned away.

One could always be sure of a ready cooked hot meal followed by a cup of delicious smelling hotly brewed tea.

On top of everything, you could see the neighborhood children sitting in her den with the twins, all cleaned and ready to have whatever goodies she was serving at that time.

Little Jim Jones one would always notice him whispering into someone's ear. This time it was Fredrick Jim said –

"These twins are surely very lucky to have Ms. Hilda as their mother. They would never be hungry Ms. Hilda loved her grands, and took great pains to protect them. They were around her continuously. She also showed much love to her younger extended families especially the males, but if asked, she would always respond with twinkles in her eyes that she loved them all.

The female extended families, they too have shown so much love for Ms. Hilda with the exception of their changling child, the one whom everyone beats upon, "Little Leca."

She was a "Little Loner." Never smiled, never cried, would stare you straight into your face, with fire in her eyes. No one got on with her, nor she with them.

She was a pretty child according to Ms. Hilda, but as the others said a "bad seed."

Let some of the antidotes be introduced to you from Ms. Daisy–

1)   One day one of the new arrivals became ill. She asked family members to take her for an emergency visit.

He had a cycle. Ms. Hilda sat on the back of this cycle – the rear back. He then advised her to hold onto the seat at the back.

She was ready. He was at first riding very slowly, but realizing he would never reach their destination, continued to increase his speed. Suddenly Ms. Hilda shouted "Oh – you are going too fast; "Stop – Stop."

He calmly explained he was going up the hill. One could imagine the pleadings that he did.

In the end he had to push her up the hill, and continued in that mode until they reached their destination.

Everyone took different areas and were waiting for them. Their were claps, jeers and laughters as they turned the corner to complete their journey. Ms. Hilda started smiling, but began chuckling, patted this young man on his hand, then told him he was naughty. Everyone laughed. That was a fun day.

As Ms. Hilda grew older she went heavily into her past. Her children's passings almost took her heart from her body.

The request she had made to the Lord while on her knees after the children's passings – "that no more young family members be taken away from her midst, until after her passing they were the last to depart for the young people for many, many years.

Even the changling child was hurt by the sad news, yet no one paid her any attention. She became very withdrawn they were the only ones who never put her down, never called her mad, crazy, or a whore. There was a big age difference, but to these younger children, that was not a problem.

Growing older, years down the changling as she was called tried very hard making connections with at least some of the senior, families to no avail.

1) One wanted her to pray for her sins.
2) Another continued to be mean
3) Another was still vicious
4) One a user
5) And one with a daughter – of – a – bitch that was the saddest misfortune one would ever come across and be in contact with, very manipulative. A borderline – who would continuously cause a lot of contention and strife in the families.

One day while bathing, there was a discussion with Ms. Hilda and one of the servants. Keeping quiet so as not to disturb anyone, as Ms. Hilda would apply "Heat for the seat," if given a chance.
This child needs a firm hand, she would never become a lady like the others. One has to mash her before she acts.
This little changling just asked for an excuse and went her way. The others kept on talking, and totally ignored her.
Ms. Hilda although an icon, was also humane

Chapter 17

Besides those that are mentioned, the others from her main blood line and their qualifications continues. Ms. Hilda had a thing about education. Everyone must be qualified. She would always say quote "You promise me degrees." She did receive them.

From her two daughters she had –

Registered nurses, government workers out of their native country, Fire Chief, Doctors, Lawyers, Teachers, Registered Nurses with teaching degrees.

Great Grands – All with Bachelor degrees, Masters, or halfway in their Masters. World soccer coaches, soccer stars representing their native country four males in number. Other cousins and extended family members know Ms. Hilda, I can now see her smiling happily as with luck all the teachings did show up.

In the end – all those early morning wakings with our books and the cane did pay off. You taught us well my lady.

Her last grand the baby of us all still remains as handsome as ever. Has turned quite a man, with two children and like the others college bond, graduated with degrees and fine jobs.

Ms. Hilda's good carma has passed on to all, along with her Dutch Blessings. Now Ms. Hilda all your wishes everyone of them have climbed their career ladders, and reached their pinacles step after step and excelled.

They have all done you proud.

And now Ms. Porta Cops – to end with your favorite poem from the middle verse

1) Who steals my purse steals trash
    it's something, nothing.
    t'was mine, t'was his, and has been slave to thousands.
    But he that filches from me my good name,
    robs me of that which not enriches him
    and makes me poor indeed.

Now your least favorite poem, showing your strengths for your family's. You did give them the gift of reading and listening

2) The boy stood on the burning deck
   whence all but he had fled
   The flame that lit the battle's wreck
   shone round him o'er the dead

   Yet beautiful and bright he stood,
   As born to rule the storm
   A creature with heroic blood

And as usual Ms. Hilda could not finish her verses.

Chapter 18

Ms. Hilda Porta-Cops was a very religious person, and had a knack for singing. Just like her slavery ancestors her strong voice of high soprano, mixed with alto always left one in wonderment. It was a wonder dear Ms. Hilda never burst one of her blood vessels.

She was close to all her extended families and friends. She maintained her respect of the Matriarch of her families close and extended, and held that unto the end.

The songs that this gracious lady loved singing were – "What a friend we have in Jesus." When the younger family members were with Ms. Hilda, they would all start in sweet refrain, even if some extra words were added, as Ms. Hilda had a way with being forgetful.
They started off with –

What a friend we have in Jesus
Above the bright blue sky,
A friend who never faileth,
A friend who never dies.
No other friend is like him
Nor like him can compare
and in his like we pray,
"They always added their own words at these endings.
This was her favorite. She even requested that this be sung at her passing.
Another of Ms. Hilda's song in high soprano was

There is a green hill far away
Outside a city wall,
Where the dear Lord was crucified
Who died to save us all.

They would sing continuously, and at these times tears will flow from their eyes.

Nursing this dear young lady, was a pleasure. Only family members were allowed to hug and kiss her, in other words one took liberty with their own closeness.

Sometimes she would request "Speed Bonny Boat," one of her twins favorite.

To know this was the same person who was so strict, without a smile, someone who would not spoil the child, but apply heat for the seat towards one especially.

As Ms. Hilda grew older, one day she pulled one of her cousins skirt, telling her the person they had hired to care for her was ill treating her. Immediately this person was fired another volunteered to look after this kindhearted lady, who had completely changed her strict meanness. One learned a lot of things as they looked after Ms. Hilda. She thoroughly taught everyone about their ancestors, and the importance of keeping up with one's traditions, customs, habits, and with families but not living in each others pockets.

Tolerance of others was very important, also kindness, lending a helping hand, and generosity.

Ms. Hilda was true and gracious as her teachings. There was always an extra space for any stranger and hot food, lemonade with ice and sugar, lovely scones, cookies, biscuits, slices of cheese and much more.

She was known for having a lot of adoptees, and all she clutched to her heart. They were all brought up as her own, and at one time you could never differentiate who was bloodline, and who was not.

Not looking for any payment, or any favors in return, this lovely lady was cared for by all.

Although spoilt by all she did recieve in return, Ms. Hilda never forgot the shocking tragedy that took away her two babies, and pulled her down at the same time.

One could never foresee how the future would end. Dear Ms. Hilda always planned to be led gently home, without a strain, a bother, worry, nor a nuisance to any of her family members.

All she wanted was to maintain the rest of her life in –

a) peace
b) privacy
c) independence
d) and most of all her dignity

Things never go as you want them to.

Chapter 19

Remembering years ago, Ms. Hilda had some quaint ways and customs.

Whenever there was a passing in the families she carried her grieving processes for years. For example
  a) A year in black for each death. As children they wore white with a black patch-or-bows.
Heaven helps them if there were two deaths back to back making it four in one month – this did happen. Of course Ms. Hilda – the good seamstress that she was started cutting and sewing for the children and adults. The kids spoke among themselves that this would go on forever. They all vowed and prayed never to become ill to die. This was forever mourning the older generation prevailed to Ms. Hilda, pleading with her to release the children from these very long stretches of mourning She agreed after six months for the last four children's deaths. They placed these peculiarities from Ms. Hilda's side of the families.

As children it was a known fact that every long weekends all the children had to be placed at the dear lady's house for deworming medications. Those were vicious times. It was as if Ms. Hilda took pleasures in these children's tortures.

Not to for-get the week-ends of bitters, with the bitter cups, bitter barks, Epson salts, and senakots – first thing on Saturdays before breakfast. Oh the pains, these vile, bitterly obnoxious tasting things that was just place on that side of the world to finish these children.

Then came the bush tea spells. The children all hated Monday mornings when those spells started. One could smell the various bushes boiling early in the mornings from Mondays to Fridays one week a month.

Never mind pouring and placing half a tea cup with cows milk, condensed milk, evaporated milk, or powdered klim milk – this bush tea would always be black and tasteless. Oh! the things one has to go through as children.

Habits are very hard to miss. Of course the marmite hot drink once a week, or on toasted bread. I prefer mine on bread with butter, said one of the twins. Oh, times were rough some of the children said

Right behind the marmite was the yeast tea. That was the worst. It was amazing said the children, Ms. Hilda never forgets these things. Even in her sleep she could remember and tells you what you have to eat and what time.

The last week was the green tea week, that they all enjoyed.

What comes next, and very large would be what Ms. Hilda calls "the body cleansing." Yes! That dreaded body-cleansing. Thankfully this happens only on vacations for example -
a) Christmas
b) Easter
c) Summers – very long summers.
This happens two fold – First –
At the start of these famous days there was the worming and checkings by Ms. Hilda. Everyone was so happy as children, after getting over these horrible wormings.
Nearing the end of all these holidays about the weekend before school reopens, all the children comes to the big house, as it was called. There everyone would be given their own buckets with lids, names written on the outside. Early the Saturday morning, always on Saturday mornings Ms. Hilda mixes –

1) quarter glass – of castor oil – that smelly brown obnoxious thick disgusting liquid oil
2) squeezed whole orange
3) egg white beaten and mixed
4) quarter glass of stout.

By the time all that was mixed thoroughly it becomes a full glass of that awful stuff. The rule of thumbs being – after the first stool which must be seen and examined by Ms. Hilda, there would be a very large meal for everyone after using their bucket which must be emptied and cleaned by Ms. Hilda.

There was a tale circling that the twins claimed they had a bowel movement, the only thing being. They were both claiming the one bucket with that stool. That was such a blast. They both held on to sides of this big can – never mind whose stool that was. Crying and screaming and being sure their time had come for their large meal. Ms. Hilda knew her children well. Neither of them received any meal. They had to wait for each other to have a stool. That was a hectic morning. They were then ready to face the new school term, said all of the children.

Their large hot meals after they were checked consisted of –
1) cow heel soup
2) calaloo soup with beef and foo-foo
3) shrimp head pound to a powder soup with crab – the children's favorite
4) black eye peas soup with beef
5) fish head soup

All of the above with vegetables from the kitchen garden.

After all of this, these children were hardly ever sick. They were all scholars, and did well years later.

Chapter 20

What amused the family more with Ms. Hilda were her rules where visitors were concerned for example –

1) A senior cousin brought a friend whom she claimed was her serious male friend. Upon arriving to the house, this senior member placed her guest in a comfortable chair and went to seek Ms. Hilda for the great introduction. Here was what took place =-

   a) Ms. Hilda stretching her hand out in greeting, said – "How do you do."

   b) Friend – "I am fine thank you," as she shook her hand firmly in return.
   Then came the no nonsense question – They all said this would never happen to them. They all agreed.

   c) What are your intensions to my little cousin. We all choked said the children.

   d) Friend – "Nothing." with a serious face.

Ms. Hilda made an about turn went into her bedroom and returned with her sewing box in hand. As their senior cousin had department for a cool drink and slice of sponge cake in a tray to regale her guest she realized Ms. Hilda was seated in the seat next to her visitor, all she did was sat quietly with Ms. Hilda between her visitor and her.

Everyone was sniggering. That was an evening they all could not forget, said the grands. Could you believe this vain matriarch took out her sewing, and started her darning, as if she was not listening to their conversation. That was something to die for in those days.

Time as per Ms. Hilda to say goodbye - this dear lady got up placed her sewing on her chair and while humming –

"La-la-bye, La-la-bye,

La-La-bye, La-La-bye

I must sing my La-La-bye.

began closing and locking her front windows. This was telling her young cousin Leca it was time for her visitor to depart. Poor Leca, she did not know where to place her pretty face.

Everything was done to time. Ms. Hilda loved to wear her native dresses which was very lovely and fitted her well on her tiny figure. They were always long, she as usual walked gracefully with her lovely floral evening house gown, and her long lovely hair in a bun. Her grey streaks visible in the night light.

By the time she had completed her song –

"Oh Lovely peace

Oh L-ove-ly L-ove – ly peace,

Let fleece flocks the hills adore" –

She came to the window where cousin Leca was about to kiss her visitor good-night.

In a polite and lady like tone Ms.Hilda said – "goodnight son."

Shocked he replied "good night Ms. Hilda" placed his hand out which she accepted.

He then went on his way, and poor cousin Leca was left on the veranda standing hands by her sides, mouth gaping open. Not a sound was made.

No one did not know how this African ancestor could do these things in time, in tune, and always come out on top smelling like a rose, a nice plum colored one.

This gifted senior with all her peculiarities, her ancestors habits, and old time ways was much loved by all. Her antics, gesticulations and redirections were popular with her very large families.

One evening another of her cousins, this time a male was in the sitting room entertaining a female guest. First one must let you know, Ms. Hilda was very proper, and from a prestigious family background, as was said before. To her, a young lady must act like one, and not one on the streets. Of course "Okee" her young male cousin had his lady friend sitting on top of the windowsill, window ledge, and to Ms. Hilda that was a "no-no."

Here was how it went.

Ms. Hilda – " Okee!

Young Cousin – Yes, Ms. Hilda.

Ms. Hilda – "Tell your young lady not to perch on my window.

Young Cousin – Okay Ms. Hilda

Naturally she removed herself and went into her bed room.

Everyone collapsed, even to the guest. For days everyone was laughing non stop. Indeed Ms. Hilda was really funny.

Chapter 21

These older generations from the slavely immediate backgrown came with a lot of knowledge.

They had brought their customs, cultures and various habits with them. Ms. Hilda besides being a seamstress, could turn her hands into anything. She was a good organizer, and made sure the plans for the children's departure placing the traveled families stay in order.

Between her, Aunt V, and dear Ms. Dairy everything was planned traditionally long before things occurred. These things were locked up securely with only three keys.

They would frequently go through these documents, so they knew the instructions by heart.

These strong females of yesteryears.
1) Knew whom to designate where
2) Which funeral home to use for their families
3) The cookers were picked ages ago
4) Who were the emergency boarders
5) Whom to bless the cattles before preparation
6) The various seamstresses for example
a) For the dead
b) For the immediate families
c) For the other families

Then comes the continuations of their Dutch cultures, habits and plans and how to pass on these things to the younger generations, or – new bloods – as they were called in those days.
They even had the names of the –
a) Strongest grandchildren
b) The stronger grandchildren
c) The strong grandchildren

To the three big dignateries of the families, as Ms. Daisy was adopted by all. They decided that their changling female "Leca" although she appeared angry, had a heart of gold, went through a lot, but came out successful. She was a little fighter, but not friendly. The child liked to be alone, changed close friends frequently. Unknown to her, she was the chosen reluctantly, as she was a rebellious tyke, especially if she feels one was getting too close to her.

One could not help at times feel sympathy for the child at the way she was being treated, but she really did remind Ms. Hilda of one of her mother's sister. Still, besides Aunt V and Ms. Daisy, those aristocratic matriarchs all had a liking for Leca, but tried not to show it, or the child would become rambunctious. That in itself would be the start of holy war for all.

No one knows what this child really thinks about. Did she remember the ill treatments and abuses she suffered. This child never says a word, no time ever. Ms. Hilda had protected her as much as she possible could, also Aunt V and Ms. Daisy. She still strongly believe her father should have taken her when he had left. Women were different in those days, these three seniors tried not to interfere – or – see what the elder children were doing regarding redirections.

She also had Aunt V and Ms. Daisy: Ms. Hilda did not know the reason that this young child now an adult was brought on this earth, but knew she was placed here for some reason, and knew someday they would all have some sign.

To know what these three seniors did in those days, what was being done at this present time was very amazing and that was –
1) Making plans for their own demise
2) Paying ahead of time for their whole funeral expenses
3) Their wills, and divisions
4) They all requested to lie in state in their churches – as they were all outstanding members of their community

5) They all wanted the family vault to be closed after their departure. A place was left for Ms. Daisy. She was a good Sister Soldier. They all grew up together

6) Even the under aged children everything was prepared for them if anything should happen, and the seniors were not around.

They were never any bother to the younger generations. They were the last of the strong blood line of slaves.

They were gone with all of their secrets and their connections, strict multi-African back-grounds and societies. These three seniors were stickers for protocol, always looking and hungry for information about their past their blood line.

After Ms. Hilda had crossed over. Aunt V, and Ms. Daisy suddenly started to withdraw from the families. This was expected, as they were very close. Everything had changed. These two found another house "Aunt V's" where they congregated, sat with their door closed. One could still hear their giggling, and chatting even outside in the corridor.

This time the evenings were coming close. Aunt V woudl say —

"shadows of the evenings,
Steals across the sky."

and Ms. Daisy who had a way of always starting sentences when every one had stopped talking said —

"Now the day is over,
Night is drawing nigh."

As usual — Aunt V the senior of the two cleared her throat, smiled, and politely waited for Ms. Daisy to finish speaking. Outside in the corridor everyone was convulsing with laughter.

These two girls as they were called by all were too much. Things were quiet for a while. Our two young seniors continued to stay by themselves.

Chapter 22

Suddenly the younger generations noticed an extra change in the house.

The noises, laughters, and singings, had suddenly stopped. All one could hear was Aunt V's voice –

So you want to leave me.

I know you've missed your friends.

You my dearest friend and sister.

have decided to join the others.

Aunt V' took a deep breath, paused, and in a weaker tone continued.

You are tired little Sis.

You really tried to keep up with me.

So go my little bird fly away.

You tell those gals I would not be left alone.

I as the eldest have to see you go safely,

then my turn would come.

Dearest, tender, sweet Aunt V turned and kissed her dear friend whom the entire families had fallen in love with and had embraced her with love, tenderness and plenty of kisses. Now this lovely much loved family wants to cross over to be with Ms. Hilda and the others whom had passed on years ago. Ms. Daisy was in a hurry to go over. How she had missed them all. Keeping her eyes closed so she could think, worried about lovely Aunt V. She knew Aunt V was tired like her, but Aunt V was always like a nesting hen with everyone. She knew she would be the last one of all the others – this majestic queen, with her head held high, well dressed in an African solid-mauve looked a pretty picture.

Aunt V sat on her kneeling stool, whispering to Ms. Daisy said–

My young Sister, you know I love you,
Don't be afraid to go, its lovely down yonder
Just think no more diseases, tears, pains,
You are going to a place of peace and love

Just remember what we were taught as kids by the lovely teacher
Ms. Benge –

Faith and strength my dears,
faith, strength and much more.
Belief, peace, and kindness,
Now add honor and obey
And what you receive would be worth the wait,
Aunt V continued, voice strong even as she was trying to control
her sad wimpers.

Do not be afraid my darling Sis.
I would always be by your side.
Keeping vigel with you
as time goes by

Ms. Daisy tried talking, but only above a small whisper.

Thank you big Sister, thank you.
You know I have to go,
I have missed my family so much.
Please look after yourself Dearest Aunt V
Care yourself my lovely Sister,
Please keep the faith,
Our very strong faith.

From then Aunt V never left the room unless it was time for
personal hygiene, and those times she would allow the children
to enter and keep Ms. Daisy's company.

This strong soldier looked after her little sister – as she called Ms. Daisy. She cared for her, in every way, and ensured little Sis every thing was prepared, nothing was changed.

Ms. Daisy had left everything for Aunt V and the rest of the family.

These last days the house was always full of relatives, visiting to hug and kiss Ms. Daisy. She was so loved by all. The minister came on Sundays for communion and prayers for the two sisters. On Friday nights at seven o'clock in the evenings, the church choir would come for sing-a-longs and prayers. Some would stay overnight especially at week-ends, continuing to bond closer with Aunt V and Ms. Daisy

The older generations were crossing over quickly and quietly, one after the other.

They were all worried about Aunt V; she would be the last of the all greats. How would this sweet-heart respond to being alone. Aunt V excels the best, when she has visitors and is entertaining also regaling them. These two sister-friends were so close; the families' wished they could do something to protect her from this kind of selfless hurt. Dearest Aunt V hardly sleeps it appears as if she was always attending to Ms. Daisy. She was never left alone, there was always someone coming in to check every fifteen minutes just in case something was needed.

These two knew what the kids were doing, smiling together, they pretended they did not know the young generation was just coming to see if they were alright.

Chapter 23

Aunt V appeared to be in an awful hurry to speak with Leca, but never told anyone the reason for such a haste.

Nothing was said to anyone by Leca when she had left the room with Aunt V and Ms. Daisy.

things were quiet for the last couple. Suddenly there was the visitors of death. Death was very permanent. They came and liked what they saw and decided to take our two loved ones. The following was all that happened –

1) One could only hear small wimperings in the room. All one could make out was Aunt V's strong altone voice saying –

Oh the families are watching and waiting,
It's time for us both to depart.
We're going, going, going their way
That's going to make everything right

So, come in lil sister, Oh come on,
It's not good to keep everyone waiting
We're coming, coming, coming to them
So everything will come out all right.

Then came Ms. Daisy's soft murmur, as if she had almost left Aunt V said –

Look Sister, My Sister, I'm coming.
I'm ready to depart with you.
We're going, yes going, going to see,
and be with everyone there.

Now let's go my Sister, Oh Sister
the time is right to depart
We're staying, staying, staying too long,
Let's go now to see everyone there.

Death came to these two matriarchs suddenly. Without a word
or thought the grim reaper appeared, came and concurred with
these two close friends. Early in the morning one of the elder
cousins came to look after these sisters prior to early breakfast.
There upon opening their adjoining rooms, she noticed, one bed
was empty implying that Aunt V's room was quiet, and the bed
was not slept on. Realizing that these sisters/friends were together
in Ms. Daisy's room. Upon opening the door after not getting an
answer, what she saw was something she would take to her grave
forever.

Glancing over the bed she saw –
a) The quiet peace of death, and the musky scents that goes
    with it
b) Both the matriarchs appeared to be in very heavy sleep
    –
    1) Ms. Daisy lying in the fetal position on her
        right side facing the door of exit and entrance.
        Her hands – the right one under Aunt V's
        outstretched left hand. Ms. Daisy's left hand
        covers and clasps Aunt V's outstretched left
        hand.
c) Ms. Daisy had an impish smile on her lips, her tapered
    eyebrows well defined, her eyes closed in sleep. She looked
    at peace with the world
d) Aunt V's head was perched at the head of the bed with
    a pillow where her head lay. Her right hand bent at the
    elbow with the palm under the right side under her right
    cheek. She too had a twinkling on her face and her lips as
    if she was trying not to laugh, as Aunt V usually does.

e) Aunt V was sitting leaning over the bed, her bottom sitting comfortable in her rocker. Her face was close to Ms. Daisy as her lips had left their mark on Ms. Daisy's forehead. So peaceful they looked together, their faces, and relaxed bodies, tells you they were happy to depart together.

Cousin Vera who had found these seniors not breathing raised the alarm –
With tears flowing down her cheeks, hands in the air said –
Oh families do come, arise and come,
for we have lost this very sad day,
The last leaders of our units
Together in peaceful harmony.

Oh come and share with us a while
The passings of our dears who have died
Yes come and mourn and be with us
As our dear Aunts have left us now.

The house was packed with this very large family, friends and well wishers. The tears flowed. Their family pastor – who was also blood related came, too grieved to say anything. Cousin Vera was the strong one at this time. Leca luckily was instructed by the seniors about two weeks prior. What to do if anything had happened to them, never realizing death would be so soon.

The whole village came out, wailing and dressed in their clothes of yesteryears. Marching in respect from East to West, North to South, you hear quek quek for the dead with answers from all sides It was as if all of this was planned. This was a full reminder of the "Pied Piper" with every one following the leader.

Then the favorite, with a full blast of –
1) Steel Band beats
2) Bongos

3) Saxaphones

This time in different rhythms one could hear –

Oh Sina dey

Raine ah co co.

Raine ah co co, ah co, ah co,

Raine ah co co.

Oh Sina dey,

Raine ah co co.

You have never heard such lovely music the beats were in reggae form. The sound of which was very loud and fit for our departing Queens.

The African Bongos were the best from the villagers. One could say our seniors were given tributes, and receptions with very much respect.

Our loving seniors as they were called with love were the last of the greats in their era.

Leca carried out all of the information she had received from our Queens exactly as was instructed by the Aunts.

Our Queens were found at five o'clock in the morning this Saturday morning, and again like history the washing day was postponed. This was our senior's time. Everything stood still on that day. A month before both of their birthdays as they were both gemini on the 13th and 16th of June in the year Eighteen hundred and two – 1802. This was both of their assumed ages, which was whispered among everyone in their family circles.

The big affairs were as follows –

1) There was the families hosts for those that were away would need places to stay

2) Cooks

3) Sewers/seamstresses as those travellers came with clothing for repair, and to make

4) The family's carpenters for building of the two caskets. The lining would be of white silk, the outside of the

caskets would be painted then varnished with the color of lilac. The vanish presented a lovely shine

5) The handles of the caskets were made of silver. Ms. Daisy loved silver

6) The pillows for the caskets were made of white silk, just as the insides of the caskets

7) Our loved ones were dressed alike, Leca decided it was only justified as they crossed over together. One would also think that these two mischievous darlings took their time to plan their departure, going away as they did

8) Both dresses were made of white damask, and adorned with rhinestones and pearls, showing the blooms on their long dresses with the encrusted pearls and rhinestones

Chapter 24

9) The yolk of their dresses were made of gipure lace adorned also with rhinestones and pearls

10) Their head dresses were made of lined gipure lace on top and white silk at the bottom. The head-dresses were tied in turban fashioned with a very large pearl on the front of each turban, with rhinestones surrounding each pearl on the turban's front

11) Their gloves were matching with their turban, along with stockings, and slippers with covered gipure lace and one large pearl each in the center of their slippers

12) Their sleeves were made of long blown out cuffs with the same materials as their dresses, with their gloves over the bands of their dresses' sleeves

13) As usual, their receiving area in their lovely Victorian house made for these occasions was painted in lilac with the large bars in white

14) The flowers' theme were white, lilac, and green leaves for backing.

Leca never realized that people could be so artistic. There were wreaths in every shape and sizes. For example –

a) Wreaths shaped with large hearts

b) Some made with the words –
   1) "I love you" in lines
   2) The best
   3) From us all
   4) Dear aunts
   5) Home Sweet Home

These arrangements, were situated and placed to catch ones eye and attention

Leca tried to remember what she felt aunt V and Ms. Daisy was trying to tell her, when she along with the others found them in the throngs of death. She really felt those words would be good for their service as their last thoughts before departing.

Suddenly like a lightning bulb it came. After the shock, pain and hurt, one would think these two were happy as they went their way in death with togetherness. Death took them both away. Together the family said they could imagine them saying –

"Be glad for us, we waited so long to depart, and could not wait any longer. This happened quickly. We both went peacefully. Thank you all for caring for us. For that we are very grateful. Please do not cry for us. There must be no mourning or grief; for I Aunt V am the most senior of everyone was one hundred years old. I lived the longest and dear Ms. Daisy our baby was all of ninety three. The master saw it fit when he made these plans for us.

So children dears please dry your eyes. There must be no more tears, just hugs and kisses my children, only hugs and kisses, and wishing us well my dears."

Everyone agreed that, to them could our loving seniors have spoken they would have said all of the above.

Everything went accordingly to plans. Leca followed instructions that was left for her in the strong iron cannister that was used for centuries. This cannister's history was it originated from Africa, which was handed down to Ms. Hilda from her father, when she was going back to Dutch Guyana to join her mother in that country.

Leca closed the family's vault. She had applied two extra drawers for this close knit families and friends; These two were the last of our greats, Leca was talking as usual to herself. Now at this time she as the designated leader by Aunt V would have to teach the younger generations to learn about their ancestors.

Aunt V and Ms. Daisy were settlers, coming from Dutch Guyana to the country of British Guyana in South America.

With tears flowing down her cheeks Leca started to hum some favorites that she learnt during the past years, wishing they were all still here with them.

The first thing that came to mine was –
Lead me gentle home –
"Lead me gentle home father
Lead me gentle home.
There to last forever
From all earthy sins
Least I fall upon the wayside
Lead me gently, gently home."

Feeling she needed to continue to get her own closure, she started again –

Oh Sina dey
Rainey ah co co
Raney ah co co, ah co, ah co

Leca could go no further; She laid on top of her bed hugging a pillow, covering her face as she broke into tears. She cried for everything,

1) All the sadness that befelled her
2) The hurts and insults
3) The losses of those whom she loved silently
4) Her loneliness
5) The isolation that had imposed on herself due to lack of trust, that in itself was very painful

Promising herself that as this was a new beginning for everyone, all the negativities must stop. Now was the time for positive thoughts, strengths, ideas, and family orientations.

She heard someone said "Ah-hem." Right away she smiled with eyes closed; Said yes Dear Aunts, and drifted into peaceful slumber, to be ready to start a new era.

Epilogue –

These new generations of Porta Cops blood-line did adhere to the past of their grands and other many extended families of yesteryears.

The difference of these new hungry brats as Ms. Hilda would have called them, just would be on anyone backs to know everything about their past which consisted of –

a) Family backgrounds
b) Countries of origin
c) The many mixed blood of our generations they were composed of. They even claimed Ms. Hilda would have been very happy if she could have heard them
d) The meaning of –
   1) Oh Sina dey
   2) Oh ju ma
   3) The various Creole songs with their meanings along with their stories
   4) The Oku tribe – the Cameroon
   5) Liberia
   6) Congonese
   7) The Dutch involvement
   8) The Chinese, Aberigineses, Portuguese along with the Negroes – these rich melting pot's coming together
   9) The connections of Nigeria, with the other factors of the Negroes coming together
   10) The moon light stories of the –
      a) Olde hyde stories
      b) Squealing pigs at nights
      c) The mermaids and their hair waist length hair, combs and brushes
      d) The Bacoo

e) The white man on a white horse, and many other jumbies along with their after death experiences

These new generations as they were called dugged their past in different ways, means, and measures.

These such very large gatherings whenever this melting pot generations got together, they found out that each had different ideas, plans, and formations of the past, decided to get together, and tried following and tracing their genes, marriages and every informative bits they could use.

This was a very slow process, and at times took its toll on them. There were cells of every ethnicities, and skin pigments. This was very important to these young ones.

They then picked some oldies at random. A particular one was –

"Oh ju ma oh."

"This is a song of happiness, of life, of good times, and better times to come for our children and us:

"Oh ju ma oh,
Oh ju ma oh;
Oh ju ma ma
Oh, oh ke co
Kera li ah ka oh
Oh ju ma ma
Oh, oh ke co
Kera li ah ka oh
Oh na ce oh ne oh le le,
Oh ne oh le le quek key me
Nar ke ah ah ne ka ke me.

This above tune became their signature song. They made it theirs.

They had two signature song, e.g.
1. "Oh ju ma oh"
2. "Oh Sina dey."

Note – All gospels, hymns, and chorus have a connection with the congregational church – or – Church of England – also – the free church.

From Chapter one – Page 6 – Bottom paragraph –
a) One could recite the words – or sing it to the tune of – "No never alone." From Ms. Porta Cops.
-Here are the words –
"No never alone – oh no
No never alone.
You promised never to leave-me
Never to leave me alone –

Repeat chorus

One page seven [7] – second chapter –
Whimpering in a fragile state – Ms. Porta Cops sang in a flat alto voice – this congregational hymn –
"I'm but not a stranger here,
Hea-a-ven is my home.
Earth is just my dearest there
Hea-a-ven is my home

Chapter three – page 14 – 2nd chapter.
This hymn's chorus is to be sung with the tune of –
Jesus loves the little children
All the children in the world
Wither yellow, black and white
There are children in his sight
Jesus loves the little children of the world.

Chapter 4. Page 18 – First chapter

A congregational gospel song.
Sung to the tune of –
"There's a stranger at my door,
Let him in.
He has been there once before,
Let him in.
Let him in the Son of God,
Let him in the Holyone,
Jesus led him over the tresh hold,
Let him in.

Indeed, this was a beloved, important family, who did not segregate, and treated everyone as equals.
Even the news said –

"A country buries its children."
"The Great loss of the Porta-Cops.
"A Grieving mother goes in poetry"
Another one wrote a few lines about the twins and their mother's mother/grandmother. Ms. Hilda Porta-Cops of the famous Porta-Cops has again lost her children in very sad circumstances..
Twelve year old twins, whose parents died during a typhoid outbreak, has now departed to rejoin their parents.
These kind hearted young males took both parents names after their passings Pat Porta-Cops left her children in her mother's care. They were two years at their parents death. They were now Simpson-Porta-Cops – their fathers surname.

What was said by all including the newspapers –

This was not a funeral for only the Afro-Caribbeans-or-blacks-or-Negroes as was called in those days.

Everyone who knew this prestigious family, their back ground, services to the communities and counties around them.

Ms. Porta-Cops was always generous to everyone, sharing her knowledge, and also learning from others. This was a give and accept attitude which was pleasing to everyone.

The indentured servitured inhabitants who later turned citizens of that country, and selectively befriended some of its people, attended as it would show poor judgment, to the country people, also as the Porta-Cops were very important to the country's people, and the government.

Now showing trusts, calmer feelings, some sense of solidarity towards their newly formed friendships, neighbors, family ties, as now these people from the other side of the world with different skin pigments and as per the natives pale skins are co-habiting with us, bringing children into the world, and becoming life partners – also as per them – common law families.
The papers printed – as their headings
"The Last of an era"
"They have left us peacefully"
"There is now the new generation of Porta-Cops"

The large Tribune wrote a few words
"They were graceful even in death"
These two sisters departed this world in togetherness
with peace and love.
They were the greatest of the "then" generation
We now have to welcome the next generation
Would they be as strong as their past ancestors

A little about my County's Historys – the beautiful Guyana –
Now the Co-operative Republic of Guyana

Population – 705,803
Size – 83,000 Square miles
Coast line – 285 ins long

There are three main rivers in Guyana mainly –
1) Essequibo River
2) Demasara River
3) Berbice River

Some of Guyana's main fruits –
1) Banana
2) Pineapple
3) Golden apple
4) Five fingers
5) Oranges
6) Tamerind
7) Grapefruit

Main Ocean
Atlantic Ocean

Mode of transportation
1) Water – Ferry, boats, canoes, ships
2) Road – cars, buses, bicycle, vans, walking
3) Helicopter

Amphibeans –
1) Alligator
2) Caymon – cousins to alligators
3) Crocodile
4) Toad
5) Turtle

Various Fishes
1) Mercurt
2) Hassa
3) Snapper
4) Butter fish
5) Tilapia
6) Banga – Mary

Exports – Guyana's main exports are –
1) Rice
2) Sugar
3) Bauxite
4) Copper
5) Magnesium

Snakes
1) Eel – could also be a tasty dish
2) Electric eel – known for shocking one to death
3) Cobra – poisonous. Its bite would kill
4) Parrot – its color is very mesmerizing to the eyes. Poisonous in its bite
5) Comoudi – very large and big in growth. It crushes when killing, strangles and stretches before devouring its prey
6) Fer-De-Lance – most poisonous snake in the world

Guyana's Early Days
Guyana is a country of ancient beginnings, trailing clouds of history that stretches deep into aniquity.
Traces of this remote past survives even up to today. Lying deep in Guyana's jungles as secrets long buried still awaits to be decoded.
We know from archaeological investigators that the land known as "Guyana" was settled long before the "years of our Lord"
In the early 17th Century when contact between the indigenous peoples and Europeans intensified dramatically due consequences

ensured for the former. Displacements form their home lands, the dislocations of plantation society, drink, disease and warfare are combined to decimate indigenous populations. Both cultures and peoples survived and today indigenous peoples from the third largest ethnic group in Guyana.

Location –
Guyana is located on the North-Eastern shoulder of the South American continent between Latitudes 1º and 9º and longitudes 57º and 61º.
Guyana is bound by surname in the East, Venezuela in the west Brazil in the South and Southwest, and the Atlantic Ocean North-Northeast.
Climate – Tropical, hot, humid, moderated by North East Trade Winds.
Currency: Guyana dollar

There are five races in Guyana – namely
1) Negroes – now called Afro-Guyanese
2) East Indians
3) Ameridgenese
4) Chinese
5) Portuguese
Depending on the areas one would have –
a) The Afro-Guyanese-or-years ago the Negroes are in the majority
b) The East Indains
The Ameridgenese resides in the interior areas of Guyana. During the years of the "Porta-Cops" they were protected by the Guyana government as there were a very high percentage of rape performed on these timed people. They were disrespected continuously.
Guyana is a melting pot of all races.

About the Author

C. Dey was born in Guyana in South America. Also named the Guyana Republic. She resigned from teaching to care for her much loved grande. Later she emigrated to Europe where she completed her education. Later she came to the U.S.A. with her husband and family settling in the state of New Jersey. She later give birth to her lovely daughter – thus now birthing two blessed children.

C. Dey has one book published by Duance Publishings inc. The name of her first book was "Purging My Soul."

A 2nd book –
Tragedy in the Third World Country –

The Songs of Pain should be in publication very soon.

This book has brought together the countries of the then British Guyana, Dutch Guyana, Liberia, the Congo, Nigeria and the Cameroons. It comprises parts of slavery and the transferral into the New Era.

The Guyana Flag

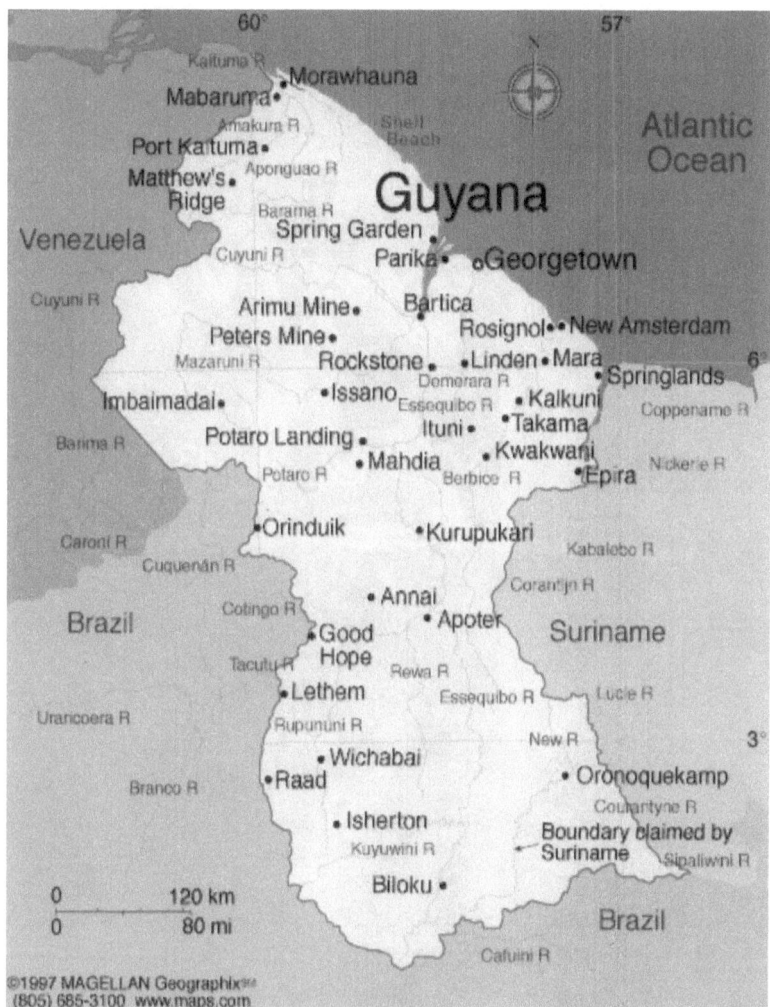

The Map of Guyana is Drawn in Bright Yellow

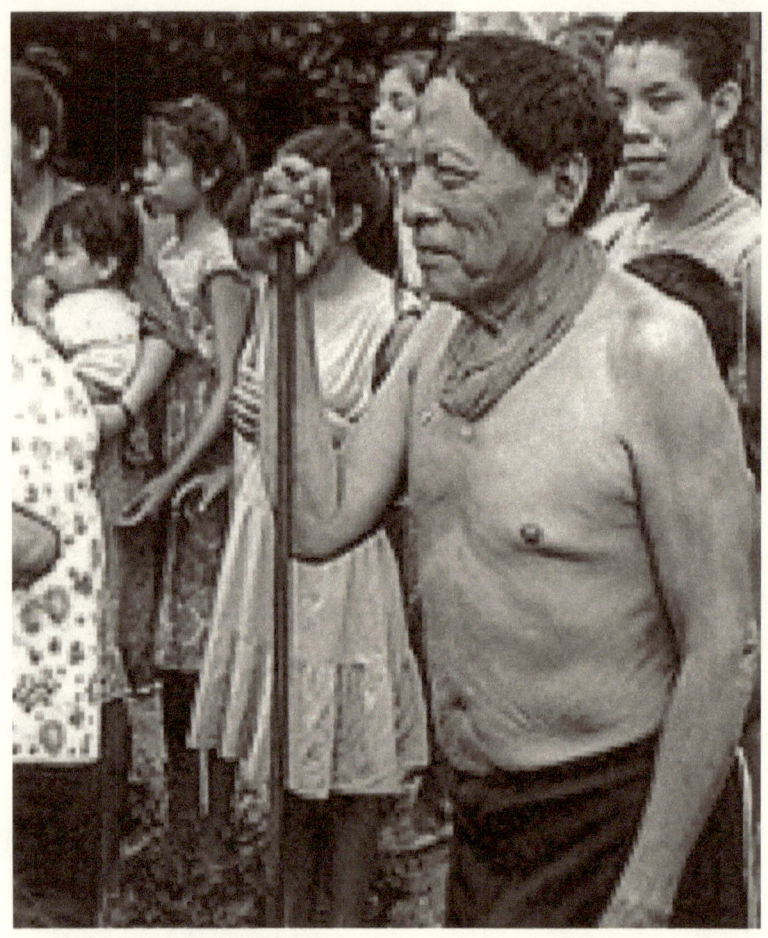

Here is an example of one of the many tribes of Guyana

Here is a market called Bourda in Guyana